D0984456

Elizabeth

Elizabeth

by
Sharon Ulrich
(with Anna W. M. Wolf)

with an Introduction and Commentary
by Selma Fraiberg and Edna Adelson

Ann Arbor
The University of Michigan Press

Contents

Introduction

Our Teacher, Elizabeth

When I first met Elizabeth she was nine months old. She was rosy and pretty and lovely to hold. When her mother or father spoke to her she broke into a beautiful smile.

I was glad to meet Elizabeth at last and I told her so. But Elizabeth was *not* glad to meet me. She put up with my testing nonsense with fortitude. But, at one point, when I took over part of the bottle feeding, Elizabeth stopped sucking, listened to my strange voice, and began to howl in outrage.

I apologized. "*You* want your mother!" I said, and quickly put her in her mother's arms. Once there, the tears stopped and she snuggled gratefully against her mother, touching her face for reassurance.

Elizabeth has been totally blind from birth. But at nine months of age, Elizabeth and a number of other blind babies were proving to us that a blind baby can love deeply and tenderly, that mother and father will be loved above all other people, and that strangers who want to find out "who is *really* important in a blind child's world" should not try my experiment again.

There is much I want to say about Elizabeth and the many blind babies we have known at the University of Michigan Child Development Project. But first let me tell you how it happened that I and a number of other people at The University of Michigan were watching Elizabeth that morning.

You see Elizabeth was our teacher. She was one of a number of babies who were teaching us about the growth and development of blind babies and young children.

We found our teacher enchanting. And distracting. There are blank spaces in our notes that morning and I think I know why. We had fallen in love with the baby, and, occasionally forgot what we were supposed to be doing. This happens to us all the time with our blind babies. When our notes are not so good we know that the baby was specially marvelous that morning and tricked us into playing games that were not on the schedule that day. . . .

I don't know what Elizabeth thought of us that morning. But in my own memory the picture that emerges is a little embarrassing. A middle-aged professor and two youngish professors are down on the floor. They take turns shaking rattles and squeaking a bunny for Elizabeth. A student assistant is moving about with notebook and pencil, now watching Elizabeth's face, now observing her hands. A photographer with a movie camera is observing *all* of us with a poker face. Whatever *he* thought of our squeaky bunny performance has never been recorded.

What were we doing there, all of us? At that time in 1966, very little was known about the development of blind babies. The National Institutes of Child Health and Development had given us funds for research, and the professors, who were crawling around on the floor with squeaky bunnies, were the research team.

I have never dared ask Sharon and Dick Ulrich what they thought of this performance and Mrs. Ulrich in her story of Elizabeth has tactfully made no reference to it. But this is surely the moment to say that if the Ulrich seniors and Ulrich juniors had not become our partners in this study, we would all be poorer in our knowledge of the development of blind infants.

What were we looking for that morning?

Many things. We were asking Elizabeth to teach us how blind babies form their human attachments. We wanted her to teach us how a blind baby substitutes sound and touch for vision in order to learn about his world. We hoped that Elizabeth would teach us how a blind baby learns to creep and

2

later to walk independently. We wanted Elizabeth to teach us how her hands would substitute for vision. We wanted her to show us how she acquired language. We wanted to learn about her sleep and feeding habits. We wanted her and all of our other babies to teach us those ways in which a blind baby's development either differed from or compared favorably with that of a sighted baby's development.

So when I picked up Elizabeth and she squirmed and strained in my arms, I knew that she was reacting to something strange in the situation, that I was an unfamiliar person. I assure you my feelings were not hurt. In this respect Elizabeth was behaving just like sighted children of the same age. When you know your mother and when love and safety and comfort are all bound up in her person, the stranger is an intruder, someone who invades the magic circle of love during this period of development.

We watched her hands as she was being comforted by mother and her hands explored mother's familiar face for reassurance. The sighted child is reassured when he *sees* mother's face and feels her comforting arms.

We were listening to her vocalizations, hard to judge in a strange environment, but what we heard was the full range of sounds that a sighted baby can make at the same age. Her mother told us that Elizabeth could imitate the sounds "Da, da," which is also within the range for sighted children. We also observed that mother talked to her a great deal, just as if the baby "really understood."

And why were the professors crawling on the floor with rattles and squeaky toys? Apart from the fact that Dr. Barry Siegel, Dr. Ralph Gibson, and I were enjoying ourselves, we were seriously at work. The rattles and the squeaky bunnies were our scientific instruments, procured by us at Woolworth's. These instruments were going to teach us how a blind baby locates objects without any other cues than sound, and how he learns to reach for and attain an object by means of sound.

If anyone had told me ten years ago that there was any point in conducting *this* experiment with blind babies. I would have been skeptical. Once upon a time I had actually believed (so did most other people I discovered) that a blind baby automatically substitutes sound for vision. After all, a school age blind child who is otherwise normal can expertly track objects on sound and recover them. But what we didn't know ten years ago was that tracking an object on sound, reaching and attaining that object on sound, is one of the most complicated tasks for a blind infant. This is not a question of intelligence. Many of the smartest blind babies we work with go through the most painful and difficult baby experiments before they finally reach the point at which they can accurately and regularly reach for and attain a desirable object.

Elizabeth at nine months eighteen days was just beginning to make tentative reaching gestures toward the rattles and sound toys that we held and sounded within easy reach. Twice in our observations, out of dozens of experiments, she waved her hand uncertainly in the direction of the sound and made contact with the object almost by accident.

But the sighted child can reach for and grasp an object between five and a half and six months! "Are blind babies retarded?" No! Within a few months Elizabeth would become expert in reaching for an object on sound. But how much learning must go into this experience for a blind baby!

Vision practically guarantees that a sighted child at five to six months will see a desirable object, will reach for it and grasp it. But for the blind child the sound of the toy "out there" is meaningless sound at five to six months. In our records we have numerous examples of very bright, very healthy blind babies at this age who make no attempt to search, even for a most favorite sound toy when it is within easy grasp!

Robbie, at six months and at eight months, is seen in our films holding his favorite musical toy, a woolly dog with a music box. He examines it, cuddles it. Then the toy drops out of his hands. It is still playing Brahms "Lullaby" and he makes no gesture of search for it! If we experiment now and hold the musical dog within easy reach of his hands while it is still playing Brahms "Lullaby," Robbie does not make a gesture of reach. And Robbie is a bright baby! But he does not yet associate the musical dog that he has just held in his hand and the sound of that musical dog "out there." It is "not the same dog" as it were. Without vision Robbie cannot yet localize sound. It is something "out there," but he has no directional cues yet. He will have to go through hundreds — no, thousands — of experiments, with one accidental success out of a hundred, before he learns that he can re-discover an object by searching with his hand. There will be thousands of experiments before he learns that the musical dog that he had just held in his hands has a separate existence "out there," — that it exists, even when he is not in touch with it.

Now this is a very complicated concept for either a sighted baby or a blind baby. But vision teaches the sighted baby and he is not required to go through thousands of futile experiments to get to this point. Even after the blind baby "gets the idea" and begins to search for and attain a toy on sound, the number of failures will be so much greater than the number of successes that we can only marvel at the perseverance of the baby. What older scientist could do as well?

Meantime, in that nine-month observation, we were looking at Elizabeth's hands with all kinds of other things in mind. The hands of a blind child must substitute for vision, but once again this is not an automatic learning for the blind infant. At nine months we noticed with great approval that Elizabeth's hands were "busy" hands. In her mother's arms her hands sought contact with mother's face, mother's mouth, mother's hands. When toys were given to her she explored the toys with interest and concentration. From her explorations of new objects we knew that she was getting a great deal of information through her fingertips. She was getting texture, shape, contours. We could guess, without even asking Elizabeth's parents, that those hands had been given a great deal of experience throughout the first nine months, experience with a wide range of interesting toys and objects. They were adept hands, too. She transferred easily from hand to hand. And when she got all the information that she could from the object in her hands we would see her sometimes bring the toy to her mouth, taste it, experience it in a new way through the sensitive lips and tongue, then remove it from the mouth and re-experience it as an object in her hands. When it was a sound making object or toy she explored it through hand movements or through squeezing the toy to create sound.

During a feeding episode when mother was giving her puréed fruit, we saw Elizabeth grab the spoon and attempt to bring it to her mouth. She made a lovely mess, of course, but her mother encouraged the attempt and took the mess goodnaturedly. After all, Sharon Ulrich was an experienced mother and she knew that all of her older sighted children had learned to feed themselves in just this messy way. When Mrs. Ulrich held Elizabeth for her bottle we watched Elizabeth's hands again. One or both hands fingered the bottle. We were pleased that Elizabeth had learned to associate the pleasures of her bottle with the cradling of mother's arms, and we were also pleased to see that, as her own hands explored the bottle, she was getting continuous information which we might describe in this way. "A bottle is something I can feel with my *hands*, slippery and slidy and rounded, and feel with my *lips* and *tongue* as I suck it and taste the milk, *and it is all these things that I experience and yet it is one thing, a bottle.*"

Meantime, too, we were using every opportunity to observe Elizabeth's posture. We saw that she was able to sit independently. At nine months this puts Elizabeth well within the range for sighted children. At another point we put her on her tummy on the floor to see what she would do. She got herself up on hands and knees which is, of course, just what many sighted children can do at about the same age. With a sighted child we would say "he is getting ready to creep" and within a very short time after the sighted child has learned to support himself on hands and knees, he "discovers" the means for creeping. Elizabeth did not yet creep in the nine month observation. We already knew from our observations of other blind babies that creeping would probably be delayed. As a matter of fact, Elizabeth did not begin to creep until thirteen months, that is, four months after she demonstrated "readiness for creeping," by sighted child standards.

But why should all of our strong and healthy blind babies be "delayed" in creeping? We got the answer through our research that very year. The answer came through an unexpected route. It did not come from watching blind babies on the floor. It came from our hand-watching study!

You remember that we described earlier the slow and difficult process through which the blind baby learns to locate an object on sound and to reach and attain that object. You remember, too, that it takes months after the blind baby makes this marvelous discovery to perfect this process of "reach on sound." Now, until we studied blind babies, none of us had given any thought to the problem of "How does the *sighted* child learn to creep?" If you had asked me ten years ago, I probably would have said, "Once he has control of his trunk and can support himself on hands and knees, he will creep. That's all there is to it." But the blind babies taught us that vision plays a very important role in creeping (or for that matter in walking, too). As we watched our blind babies poised beautifully on hands and knees and unable to creep for weeks or months, we began to ask ourselves, "What would the sighted child be doing at this point?" And then a picture emerged.

The sighted child is on his hands and knees practicing rocking back and forth in this position for a few days or at most a couple of weeks. One day he sees an attractive object just out of reach and he makes a lunge for it. (He has been expert at reaching for and attaining objects since he was six months old). Now the reach for the out-of-range object pulls him forward. With the first attempt he will probably fall flat on his face. Then he gets up again on his hands and knees, makes another reach and collapses. But he is getting closer each time to his prize. Once again, up on hands and knees, he moves a little forward and this time he has it! Within a few days this "reach and collapse" technique is replaced by a coordinated movement of arms and legs and the sighted baby, lured on by wonders all over the place, begins his travels on all fours.

But the blind baby poised nicely on hands and knees at nine months has not yet learned to accurately locate, reach, and attain an object on sound alone. Or, if he has begun his tentative and uncertain reaches (as we saw with Elizabeth) he will not master the art for several months. And so it happens that an old fool like me once spent fruitless sessions trying to lure Robbie to creep by placing his favorite musical dog within a few feet of the baby while he was nicely balanced on his hands and knees. Nothing happened. Robbie did not reach for the dog although he seemed attentive to the old melody of Brahms' "Lullaby."

But when Robbie was eleven months old and was able to reach for and attain a sound object Robbie began to creep! At this point the sound object became a lure in the same way that the sight of an attractive toy becomes a lure for the sighted child!

We discovered through repeated examples in our research why the blind child is "delayed" in learning to creep. For similar reasons the blind child may be "delayed" in independent walking. But this "delay" has nothing to do with intelligence. Elizabeth, whose good intelligence will speak for itself in her mother's story, learned to creep a little later than sighted children and learned to walk a little later than sighted children.

Do blind babies sleep more than sighted babies? By the time I saw Elizabeth at nine months she was down to two one-hour naps in the course of the day and slept from 7 p.m. until 5 or 6 a.m. This puts her sleep pattern entirely within the range for sighted children. Through our study of many other blind babies we have learned that the blind baby who finds his world "interesting" during his waking hours (and his parents have a great deal to do with this) follows the same sleep pattern as that of a sighted child.

Is the blind child "fussy" about his food? Does he have difficulty with solids and chewing? Elizabeth was a hearty and enthusiastic eater, she accepted solids, began to chew her food at the same age as the sighted children do, and her parents have never reported a feeding problem. While parents and educators of blind children have described special difficulties in these areas, we found that nearly all of the blind babies we followed from birth went through normal phases of sucking, chewing, and swallowing, when the normal opportunities were offered to them by their mothers.

We followed Elizabeth throughout the early years of her development. Mainly we made home visits and occasionally Elizabeth visited us at our Project office. She got to know a number of the senior staff members in our Project. There was Barbara Wasylenki, Marguerite Smith, Evelyn Atreya and, of course, Edna Adelson who was in touch with Elizabeth and her family throughout most of these early years and who was largely responsible for encouraging Mrs. Ulrich in the writing of this book.

On our visits to Elizabeth and her family we observed, we recorded, we filmed regularly so that all of us on the Project staff could share the experience of watching her development. Mr. and Mrs. Ulrich shared all of their own observations with us. They were first-rate observations too! For our part, we could share our own developing knowledge of the growth and development of blind young children and, where our experience might be useful in problem solving or in understanding, we offered information or suggestions which the Ulrichs could use or not use as they saw fit.

But now we are a bit ahead of the story. We left Elizabeth on the floor at nine months of age. We could not yet know what Elizabeth would teach us. Nor could we know what our many other babies would teach us. Elizabeth would teach us that a blind baby under certain favorable circumstances, would form deep and enduring human attachments, that she would find substitutes for vision in learning about her world. She would show us that her hands would become marvelous instruments for exploring and learning; that she would walk, run and climb; that she would match any sighted child in speech; that she would have playmates (including, later, imaginary playmates), that she would get into mischief, that she would hold her own in a sighted nursery school, that she would acquire independence in dressing and feeding and in asserting her rights.

She would achieve a very large number of the developmental accomplishments of a sighted child. But the most important thing that Elizabeth and our other blind babies have taught us is this: *The blind child must find his way to these accomplishments by routes that are very different from those of a sighted child.* To travel a developmental road in darkness means many pauses, many detours, much help from devoted parents. But even the most loving parents of a blind child may not find the pathways because all the roads look different in the dark! All the signposts that parents can read for their sighted babies are missing.

And so it happens, very often, that the baby in darkness is guided by two parents who love their blind child and are often lost themselves in a maze of unmarked routes, wrong signals. There are no signs that can be read as "Slow down," "Curve," "Detour," "Stop," "Go," "Alternate Route #56," "Rough Road Ahead," "Smooth pavement 100 yards."

Our work at the Project with many babies finally provided us with a map to the uncharted route. We learned where most of the road blocks were and how the baby might find the detour or be helped to find the detour by his parents or by us. And as more babies were brought into the study and the landmarks were charted by us, our scientific study could now be used to benefit blind babies and their families.

With the generous support of the Office of Education, Bureau of the Handicapped, we began another program in which our research findings were translated into an educational program for blind infants and their families. Our staff of trained baby specialists provided home consultation for families with blind babies and young children. We visited twice monthly, always hoping of course that the baby and his family would come to us as soon after birth as possible. We helped our parents to understand the extraordinary problems in development of blind babies and children and how to provide the necessary support and experience that will promote healthy development. We shared with our parents our own understanding of their baby and we found, to our great satisfaction, that when parents understood the experience of a blind baby and young child, they became wonderfully inventive in helping their baby find his way.

We helped our parents to understand how the blind baby made his human attachments and how mother's or father's voice and touch could substitute for vision. We helped our parents to understand the special needs of the blind child in obtaining rich experience through his hands. We experimented with toys, and for two years the Women's Psychiatric Auxiliary of the University of Michigan Medical Center carried on a toy project with us and our parents. We adapted many of the readily available infant and pre-school toys and designed some toys for our blind babies which might enrich the tactile experience of the hands, or unite touch and sound in special ways.

We were on hand to share the parental anxieties at each of the turning points on the road when the blind baby's path makes a detour. At five months: "Why doesn't he reach for his rattle?" "Why doesn't he search for his squeaky bear?" "Is he deaf?" "Is he retarded?" We could explain the detour, allay the anxieties, and help the parents to build in the experiences that the baby would need between five months and perhaps twelve months when his hands would begin to make a sure reach for a sound object. Or at ten months: "Why isn't she creeping?" "All she can do is rock back and forth on her hands and knees. Is she brain-damaged?" "Is she retarded?" "Will she ever walk?" And if we knew on good medical authority that the baby was otherwise healthy, and if our own assessment showed a normal progression for a blind infant, we could help the parents understand the delay and the detour. Then one day there is a telephone call and the news is telegraphed from one staff member to another, "Karen is creeping!" "Paul walked across the room for the first time!" And now we prepare ourselves for a series of complaints from parents. They

11

sound very familiar to the parents of sighted children. "He's into *everything!*" "I can't take my eyes off him for a *moment.*"

I remember the terrible concerns of Robbie's parents at nine months and their fears that he might never walk. One of my fondest memories is a picture of Robbie at the age of two racing down the slope behind his house with a devilish grin on his face, while his mama panted in her pursuit, thirty feet behind him, hoarsely calling his name.

We discovered, early in our work, that the most important gift we could bring to the parents who were working with us was "Hope." No, not hope of vision, ever, for most of the babies, but hope that this blind baby would grow into a full-sized human being, loving and fun-loving, capable of deep feelings, independent in walking and self-care, speaking well, playing, learning in school, going to college, becoming self-supporting, getting married, having children.

Some of our parents had been without hope. Many parents thought that a blind baby would have to be mentally retarded. Some parents thought that a blind child would always be helpless. Few of our parents imagined or could imagine the future of their child.

Many times we wished there were some way to show our parents a picture of a blind child's early development. When Sharon Ulrich told Edna Adelson of our staff that she was writing the story of Elizabeth it struck all of us that no one could speak more directly to parents of a blind baby than parents who have lived through the experience themselves. When Mrs. Ulrich showed us the early first draft of her manuscript we felt that the story of Elizabeth, as told by her mother, was one that should be shared with other parents of blind infants, with the educators of blind children and, equally important, with all those who care about children blind or sighted. For editorial help to Mrs. Ulrich we suggested Mrs. Anna Wolf, whose lifelong experience in both parent education and editorial work is widely known. Edna Adelson of our staff worked closely with both Mrs. Ulrich and Mrs. Wolf. Both of us, representing the Child Development Project, read chapters and occasionally complained that *our* favorite stories of Elizabeth had been accidentally omitted here or there. Following Mrs. Ulrich's story, Mrs. Adelson's story will lead us back into the psychology of the blind infant and young child and to the early education of the blind child as we see it in our work at the Project.

Among all the things that Mrs. Ulrich's story can bring to parents, there is a message that only a personal story can bring to other parents who may be struggling with their own pain at the first discovery of blindness in their baby.

Mrs. Ulrich can speak of her own grief and her husband's with some perspective now, yet, even in the writing we know that the remembering of this pain renewed it. . . . A baby is born and everyone is delirious with joy. Then, some months later, there is the discovery that the baby is blind. There is shock and a grief so terrible that it cannot find words for a long time. In Sharon Ulrich's story we are permitted to share the grief which, I think, she could not have shared with us at the time. From her story we understand that there was deep love between these two parents and that their sharing of pain brought consolation and finally a healing of the wound.

Sometimes in our Project work we have met two young parents, new to marriage and to each other, new to parenthood and new to grief of such dimensions. At such times grief may open old wounds. Self-blame, blame of each other, all the old ghosts that live in all of us may rise to the surface to add to the torment. And while it is easier to bear pain when "blame" can be assigned, it will not end the pain and it postpones the healing. No one is to blame for the blind baby. Those young parents who put away these self-torments, found ways to comfort each other, and their own love was strengthened.

Mrs. Ulrich's story begins, as every such story begins, with pain and the overcoming of pain. And it ends (for this book only, of course) with Elizabeth in school, full of promise, a merry, self-confident, intelligent and most endearing child who is certain to have her full share of all the good things in life.

Selma Fraiberg,
Professor of Child Psychoanalysis and
Director of the Child Development
Project; Department of Psychiatry,
The University of Michigan Medical School

We were expecting another baby. We understood, or thought we did, that in bringing a child into the world, parents always assume some risks. Though ordinarily these are small, in our case the risks were somewhat greater than for most. Yet thus far, fortune had favored us, we had four healthy children. Then, out of the blue, one of those disasters that "happen only to other people," struck us. Our Elizabeth, our fifth child, was blind.

I

Beginnings

Today at nearly five years of age, Elizabeth is a happy active
child full of curiosity about the whole wide world. She walks
with a confident gait, talks well and is a lovely songstress. She
is learning to take her place with family and friends and to
hold her own. This past year, she has attended a nursery school
for normal children and done well. But because the early
months of a blind child's life are so crucial, I want to go back
to the beginning, to tell how it all happened.

She was born prematurely, six months after conception,
and weighed just two pounds four and a half ounces. It had
been six months of wondering whether I would be able to
bring this new child to life, for I was one of those women
who had difficulty carrying a pregnancy to full term. Two of
my older children were premature.

As I lay on the delivery table I heard the doctor say, "A
little girl. She seems all right but she is very small."

He asked the nurse to bring the holy water so he could
baptize her and I saw a tiny purplish baby in his hand. Then
they put her in an isolette and presently wheeled her to my
side so I could see her. Oh God, how small! Smaller even
than my son Mark had been!

In a few days I was strong enough to go home, but
without Elizabeth. Though she was "holding her own," I was
told that she must weigh five pounds before she could be ours.

Every day in the two months that followed I called the

17

hospital to check her weight. At first she lost a little. Then began the slow gains.

One day the doctor called to say that Elizabeth's heart had developed a murmur. They were giving her digitalis and some more oxygen. I knew that premature babies usually need some oxygen and that the amount must be carefully regulated. Too much is harmful, but maybe this extra amount was necessary to save her life.

The trouble passed, the heart grew stronger, and she neared the five-pound mark. When Elizabeth was just short of that tremendous weight, we were told we could take her home.

At home I had a wonderful friend named Rose. She came into my life, when I was pregnant with Elizabeth, as a household helper and though after I came home from the hospital we no longer needed her to work for us, she has remained a friend of the whole family. When I got that call saying we could come to the hospital and take our baby home, I put my arms around Rose and gave her a big hug before dashing to the phone to call my husband. Together, he and I brought our baby home.

We laid her on the bed and unwrapped her and she seemed to us absolutely perfect. Now two months old, she smiled at us and Lord, how beautiful she was! Her brothers and sisters gathered around in fascinated awe—she seemed to them so tiny. I told my son Mark that he was just that size when he came home. The next morning we spread pads and soft blankets on the kitchen table and gave her a bath and I went about it feeling smug and confident. I had been waiting two months for just this, convinced that no matter how good the care of babies may be in hospitals, I could do a better job. I revelled in stroking baby cream on her body, talking to her, kissing her toes, her fingers and even her small bottom.

Two weeks later, I took her to the pediatrician. She had gained weight, seemed contented and active. Later, at her three months check-up, the doctor said she was perfect.

I was relaxed and happy with my wonderful family. I had five beautiful children—Terese, Mark, Sharon, Dickie, and now Elizabeth. We had recently moved into our present lovely home, spacious enough for our large family and on two acres of land in a small country town near a larger city. My husband's business prospered. He is a grower, buyer, and shipper of onions, and also trades in stocks on the Commodity Board. Best of all, I know I can always count on his understanding and strength in time of stress. It seemed to me that not a person in the world could be more blessed than I.

The Ordeal

The time came for Elizabeth's four months check-up. Usually my husband went with me on these visits. This time, he was busy and I assured him I could manage by myself. Having arrived at the doctor's office, I waited for my name to be called, entered the examining room, and watched while the doctor did the routine things. Then he began to check her eyes with unusual care and I could see he was concerned. Finally, he handed me the instrument, directing me to look through it at Elizabeth's eyes.

"Do you see that white mass?" he said. "We look for this in babies as premature as Elizabeth. I think you should have her seen by an ophthalmologist. He can advise you better than I can." He went to the phone and made an appointment for us then and there.

The week of waiting for that appointment was agony — a week of staring into Elizabeth's eyes, of trying all sorts of tests to show that she could see. Nights were filled with waves of awful foreboding. Finally, just before Christmas, when the whole world was crisp with snow and people all around us were busy and merry, we drove into town for that appointment.

But within myself, I already knew what the verdict would be. The specialist and his assistant again went over Elizabeth's eyes. They were very thorough and though they were kind, it was hard on Elizabeth and she cried. They would say, "Easy tiger, easy tiger," until the ordeal was finally over and I could again hold and comfort her. Then, as it seemed to me in the far distance, I heard the word "blind" and the doctor was saying that, hard as it seemed, she "would never know the difference."

Numbness spread over me. All this had no reality even though, in another part of myself, I had known it before they spoke.

The next day I broke out with hives. Without my conscious mind knowing how violently I was feeling, somehow my body knew. There I was — calm enough on the outside, but inside, a world was collapsing and taking its toll. The first thing I did was to seek help and consolation from my family doctor. I showed him my case of hives and told him what the specialist had said about Elizabeth. My doctor has always been a great friend. Though at first incredulous, he shared my mounting grief.

He gave me a shot to relieve the hives and a pill to relax me, but all the way home there was a painful tightness in my throat and the ache seemed to spread to every part of me.

We had been advised to seek even further help—this time at the University of Michigan Medical Center in Ann Arbor. When the day came, my husband readied the car, I packed Elizabeth's bottles and diapers, gave household instructions to the other children and kissed them good-bye. It is a two-hour drive from our home to Ann Arbor and we drove silently, both of us wrapped in our private thoughts. Today, those thoughts are as vivid as the most recent events. They rush in like ocean waves and, like the shells left behind, so are my memories.

I recall that before the first doctor's examination, I had never noticed anything wrong with Elizabeth's eyes. She seemed to me quite perfect. But after the visit to the specialist my fears took over. I remembered how I had kept testing and retesting her, how I had held her near the Christmas tree hoping she would notice the glittering lights, bringing her close to those lights, searching her eyes for a response, a change of expression. There was none; no happy little wiggles at discovering something new and pretty. But I had somehow kept on hoping and fooling myself. "Yes she can, no she can't" went my thoughts. For a time, we believed she responded to light and dark, but after awhile, that too seemed to disappear. I noticed also that her eyes seemed to wander more than most babies'.

At the University Hospital, it took the doctor just fifteen minutes to tell us our baby was blind. This is what he said.

"Your baby is blind. There is nothing we can do for her. The condition is called retrolental fibroplasia and is a result of the oxygen given her at birth." The young intern who was there during this examination kept his eyes averted most of the time but glanced at us briefly now and then when he dared to. It was a look compounded of compassion and embarrassment — a look which I have now seen from strangers many times. But the people in the waiting room who did not know, looked at us as we left and smiled. "What a cute baby," one of them said.

Then something happened that was truly good, though at the time I could not possibly know just how good it was to be. We were taken to Mrs. Fraiberg's office at the Child Development Project in the Department of Psychiatry at the Medical Center. This is a research project studying the development of babies blind from birth but otherwise undamaged. Though the name sounds formidable, the workers we talked to were truly warm and understanding. They asked if we would be willing to bring Elizabeth to Ann Arbor once a month for a while, so that they could observe her development. They would also answer any of our questions and give us advice if we wanted it. Naturally we said yes, especially when we learned that this is the only existing systematic study of infants blind from birth. We were told that Elizabeth with proper training could develop normally and that what we learned would be made available to guide other parents with babies like ours. Much, we were told, has been written about the school-age blind child, but by then, the help given may already be too late for good results.

So with our first slight ray of hope we returned home.

Dear Rose was sitting at the kitchen table with the four older children waiting for our return.

Before I begin the story of how we helped Elizabeth so that today, except for some permanent accommodations to her blindness, she is a normal child among normal children, I want to make it clear that we first had to begin with ourselves. Now finally, facing our problem alone, there were the inevitable slumps.

Yes, we raged inwardly at the doctors and the hospital staff for giving too much oxygen. Cases like Elizabeth's were almost nonexistent because the cause of her condition was known, the importance of proper regulation of oxygen well understood. Did a shortage of staff, a problem in most hospitals, lead to negligent monitoring? Did the heart murmur that developed really require that extra oxygen to save her life? We will never know. Doctors make mistakes like the rest of us. They also protect each other from disclosure of mistakes.

Sometimes I blamed myself for starting another baby when the odds were strong that it could be premature. I argued with myself that I had nevertheless always come through pregnancy with a healthy child. Worst of all was the suspicion that I was feeling sorry for *myself*. Could it be that I resented this blind baby? Was pity for myself greater than my pity for her? Both my husband and I had to admit to ourselves that, yes, there were times when this was true. Yet when I looked into the faces of our other children and into their clear blue eyes that could *see*, my heart ached just for Elizabeth and the self-pity vanished.

I must also admit that communication with neighbors was hard for me, though I am sure they meant well. In our small community, news spreads fast. People felt they had to say something and they seemed to strike the wrong note. I hated the studied cheerfulness, the insistence on the "bright side."

"She doesn't look blind," they would say. Or, "It could be worse; she will never know what she has missed." In those days, we could not imagine anything worse. Or "You take it so wonderfully," they said. How did they expect me to take it? — shout my agony to all comers?

I don't know just when or quite how it happened but after a while the agony, the anger, the self-pity, the guilt feelings grew less. And I could accept the neighbors' well-meant words as kindness. Together, my husband and I seemed to arrive at a point where we bent our wills to the hard work ahead and saw it as a challenge and, yes, a "call." Somehow we would manage to work it out. The shift was very gradual. There still came times when I wanted to shove the whole business away and make someone else carry the burden. I had to force myself to live just one day at a time, and some days were good and some were very bad. Though the bad ones have grown fewer, I know now that they will recur occasionally as long as I live, and I have found relief in accepting this. After all, I am a human being, imperfect and fallible. This realization has helped me to quit blaming myself and others too. It helps today when I look at Elizabeth to feel not only overwhelming love but pride too.

Our religion has been a deep source of help for us both. Though we are not what you might call "pious," our belief in God and the power of goodness has helped us chart our course. We believe too that we are never sent trials without also the strength to bear them. When friends tell me they never could have faced such a problem as we have had, I say to them, "Of course you could. We can all do what we have to do." A fault of mine—I tend to get impatient with self-pity and must remind myself that I, too, have had such moments.

So today, I can still say as I did when we first brought Elizabeth home — "I have been greatly blessed."

Wake Up and Live, Elizabeth

So we set to work to help Elizabeth grow into a normal human being.

It was fortunate that she was not our first child. As parents of four, we had had experience; and perhaps I had developed a kind of knack with children. Also, the people from the Project were a great help. Though their purpose was to observe and record Elizabeth's progress, they also gave me some good ideas when I asked for suggestions; and they were so obviously pleased with Elizabeth's progress that after their visits I was always more secure about being on the right track.

I seem to have known instinctively that even a newborn baby needs holding and cuddling and talking to; and that feeding time offers special possibilities for this. There can be real communication between mother and child at this time as she watches closely and picks up the cues he gives her. Is he more comfortable held this way or that? Does he want the bottle this very minute or does he want to take some time off and just rest or squirm and look around a bit? He'll "tell" you if you "listen."

Two premature babies before Elizabeth had taught me that they may, at first, resist cuddling. They are stiff and unrelaxed because they have had weeks of lying on the hard surface of an isolette where they are handled as little as possible to avoid infections. If a mother doesn't realize this, she may feel disappointed when her baby seems to prefer the crib to her arms and appears all too willing to have the bottle just poked in his mouth at feeding time. Elizabeth was like that at first — was worse even than my son Mark, having been in the hospital a whole month longer. When she first came home, instead of cuddling in my arms, she would rear up in protest. But I was determined not to give up, convinced that this early rapport between mother and child is the very foundation of both learning and loving.

I slowly and gently pushed her down into the crook of my arm, taking lots of time about it, and so gradually induced her to take the bottle. Her acceptance and responsiveness to me, I felt, was even more important than how much milk she took. So if she said no thank you to the bottle, I would just hold her and chatter to her a bit, rock her or sing to her. Gradually I won her. She began to settle in my arms,

24

smiling back at me and answering all my talk with happy gurgles.

At about six months, I was rewarded. She began to be distinctly partial to me, responding with a special smile to the sound of my voice and turning her head in my direction when she heard it. I believe the beginning of something we call "love" starts with the strong preference of the child for the mother. It must be accepted as part of normal emotional development even though it brings some inconveniences.

By ten months of age, Elizabeth definitely wanted only me. In a pinch, she might permit the ministrations of Rose or my oldest daughter Terri, but she would have nothing to do with anyone else. This is hard on Grandmas and others but it works itself out, I have found, if you don't push.

Somewhere between a year and a year and a half, Elizabeth could tell by the tone of my voice when I disapproved of something she did and began to comply when I said "No, no, Elizabeth." She also reached out to me joyously when I entered the room or when I was tending her. And when she began to creep, she could locate me by sound and followed me across the room.

All this means that if a mother has to be away from home, as can happen, much thought should be given to leaving her baby in the care of someone she knows and is used to, even if that person is only second best.

When Elizabeth was seventeen months, I had to go to the hospital for an operation; but I felt comfortable about leaving her with Rose whom she had known from the beginning. Every family should have such a friend they can call on at such a time. As it worked out, during my nine days in the hospital, there was a tremendous snow-storm. Even the doctor was marooned in the hospital for three days and Rose couldn't get to our house. However, by the same token, neither could my husband get out, and the children's school was closed. So everyone stayed home and Elizabeth had all the people around her she knew best. When finally the family could get out, Rose could come in, so all was well. They reported that Elizabeth seemed contented and happy. However, I have to confess that later on, when Elizabeth was about 20 months old her "mother fixation" reached its height; she could hardly let me out of her "sight"! I do not know whether this was connected with my having been away but she eventually worked out of it.

If this phase of development is hard for a sighted child, how much harder it must be for one who is blind and has fewer avenues of reassurance that mother still exists.

There is something else I believe applies to both blind and sighted children. It is not necessary to slap their hands when they touch forbidden objects. Especially, this applies to a blind child. Elizabeth's *hands are her eyes*—and who would ever slap a child in the eyes! I teach my children whenever possible how to handle things safely and if there is too much risk, I put all those valuable or dangerous things away until the day comes when the children can be depended on. That way I'm not eternally yelling "no" and getting out of temper.

We had heard, of course, of the special importance of exposing blind children to the feel of a variety of objects — hard, soft, large, small, and so on; also to different textures, such as varying grades of sandpaper, to velvet, burlap, corduroy. This helps them make full use of their sense of touch and prepares them for the bumps of Braille later on. But, as with all children, common household objects are also indispensable teachers. We all know with what joy a child gets into the kitchen cupboards and the wonderful "toys" he finds there. There are always those family-room tables loaded with magazines, ash-trays and what-nots. At a glance, the sighted child sees what's there. Lacking the sense of sight, the blind child, however, must use everything he has to come to understand them. This is essential to his discovering that there is a great world outside his own body. He begins then, to differentiate between "me-*here*" and "many-other-things-out-*there*." Instead of becoming turned inward and tragically limited by his blindness, he feels the healthy urge to get out and explore.

Like other small children, Elizabeth soon began to put

everything in her mouth. Though I had accepted much of this in my other children, I found that Elizabeth needed to do this even more and for a much longer time. I gave her complete leeway with this. She was free to mouth everything to her heart's content, for I knew that lips as well as fingers could help her learn. Such learning is all a much slower process with a blind child. One must do a good deal of planning. Fewer things can be left to chance. As soon as Elizabeth could sit with support, I put her in a chair at a table with many objects on it and a rail to prevent their falling off. I explained to my other children that play with Elizabeth should be a learning experience whenever possible and the reason why. Once accepted, we could adjust to the slower pace and rejoice together at each new forward step.

It was also very important for us to learn not to push too hard. We were not formal about our "lessons." We didn't make her perform set tasks at fixed times. When she seemed tired or fretful, we let her pass on to something else — or just do nothing for a while. We settled for small gains.

Reaching for the World

So much for general principles. But practical applications are of great importance.

I knew that if Elizabeth were to learn to move about and eventually walk she must have incentives. Sighted children are provided with such incentives largely through vision. First they begin to reach out for what they want, making all sorts of random movements before they learn to contact it quickly. If it is out of reach, they try humping themselves toward it; then they discover there are even better ways to get places, such as creeping. Finally they stand on their two feet and walk. I realized that if Elizabeth was ever to reach out and live in the world, she must discover as soon as possible that there were interesting things outside her own body which she could feel, hear, taste, smell, then learn to locate and finally reach for and retrieve.

Before I knew that Elizabeth was blind, I had bought her a set of plastic bells as a Christmas gift that first year. On the fateful day when we arrived home from Ann Arbor in full knowledge of what we were facing, I strung those bells across her bassinet near enough so that if she raised her arms just a little she would be bound to make contact with them and hear their tinkle. For a while, she hit them purely by accident but soon she appeared obviously pleased at the sound and purposely reached out and knocked them to and fro. Hearing and feeling those bells had to take the place of seeing them. It took her longer than it would a sighted child to discover that these lovely things were *out there*, but eventually she did and her hands searched for them.

I put other objects around her too; and when she was about four months old I had her lie on the floor and put many things around her — sponges, rattles, plastic spoons, and also a small dinner bell for sound. I put a rattle into her hand and then guided it to her lips for further exploration. If she dropped it, I would rattle it where it was, then guide her hand to it, clasp her hand around it and guide it again to her mouth for her to feel. I did this sort of thing over and over with her for perhaps fifteen or twenty minutes at a time for a good part of her waking moments, making sure she had experiences that involved hearing, tasting, feeling, smelling, and so was learning to locate objects through the use of all senses. When she seemed tired or had had enough, I took her on my lap and rocked or sang her to sleep.

Sometimes during "lessons" I held her on my lap and rang the bell from different directions to see if she turned her head toward it and after a while, she did. Or, I would drop the bell on the floor and soon she got so she leaned over toward it in response to the tinkle.

When Elizabeth was nine and a half months old she really could reach directly for an object on sound-cue. Then I would just stand near by and watch her, talking to her encouragingly and when she finally found it, said "Hurrah, you've got it!", and gave her a big hug and kiss. It was pure fascination.

Of course I acquired a lot of very special toys for her too — blocks that rattled, a musical teddy-bear, a doll. They were all right; she liked them for a time, especially the ones that made a noise, but she often ended up with such things as her brother's steam shovel, his cards, or my pastry brush. And she just loved a big piece of wax paper to rattle. Special equipment isn't absolutely necessary at this age, I found. What's needed is imagination in using the common objects all around.

At this time, the whole family took turns at playing little games with Elizabeth. We did such things as "pat-a-cake," "this little piggy went to market." We played "horsey" on our legs, by the hour, so it seemed, believing that the up and down motion was a bit new and might give her the idea of a three-dimensional world, while teaching her that she could be safe even with her feet off the ground.

All this time, Elizabeth was definitely learning to move around on her own.

She turned herself over when she was five months old.

Around six months, she began to roll over and over across the room until she was finally stopped by bumping into something. Clearly she was gaining more and more control of her body and was eager to use it.

When she was eight months old, I got her a baby chair with a railed tray for toys and, when she seemed ready, I put her in without pillows to prop her so she would learn to use her own muscles to sit erect. She rebelled at first but later caught on. At nine months, she was sitting fairly well and soon could also raise herself from lying prone to a "bridging position" on hands and knees. So I then put her on the floor to play, placing a pillow on each side of her as well as in back so she wouldn't be frightened if she toppled over. The time comes when a child can profit from a bump or so — but to begin with, he needs some protection.

When she was ten months old, Elizabeth could sit and

topple over and pick herself up to a sitting posture again without developing fears.

At just under eleven months she could stand when someone held her hand or, when holding onto a rail, could even take a few faltering steps.

Elizabeth was around a year old when she began to creep. I had thought the day would never come. I had tried to teach her by putting her on all fours and getting her to move first an arm, then a leg. But she always went flop. Clearly, she was going to creep only when she got good and ready. Finally, the day came when she rose to her hands and knees, rocked back and forth, moved first a leg and then an arm and so started the great act of setting forth into the world!

Soon after Elizabeth started creeping, I found her one morning standing up in her crib. After that, I put her in a playpen so she could practice standing and learning to walk around the pen holding on — another step toward independence and self-confidence. Finally, I got her out of the pen as often as possible and let her explore pretty much on her own all around our family room.

When this free creeping began, I had the impulse to clear a path for her. Then I changed my tactics and just said, "Elizabeth, be careful," and she learned to stop and feel for what was in her way. I got the other children to understand the importance of not making everything too easy for Elizabeth but also of keeping a watchful eye for whatever might be too dangerous. This kept us hopping! It takes judgment based on close knowledge of a particular child to decide when he can go it alone; and there are times when you hold your breath.

Elizabeth had a couple of falls, including one hard bump when she really cried. What child doesn't? But I can say that she has actually had fewer mishaps than my other children. She moved and still moves more slowly, feeling her way as she goes, but she does not move timidly.

When Elizabeth was 16 months old and was creeping but not yet walking, we made a big investment and bought for her an indoor slide which we kept in our family room. We thought she might just like cruising around it and enjoying this large new object to *feel* long before she could really use it. But to our gleeful surprise, within a month, she was crawling up the slide part and soon after, the steps. This too kept us hopping because what went up couldn't always come down — alone, that is. "Watch her," I would call to the other children and when Elizabeth began to talk, she would echo "watch her!" as she started up the slide.

Today, that slide is in use much of the time. It has developed her self-confidence as well as enjoyment of all the new tricks it makes possible.

Elizabeth was usually with me when I worked in the kitchen. What fun it was to dump the cereal on the floor and lie in a delicious mess of crispy crunchies. I let her do such things much longer than I had permitted such messing from her brothers and sisters. It meant more work for me but progress for Elizabeth. My own order of priorities had undergone radical changes. Order, neatness and such matters took their place way down the list.

All this time, I kept my contact with the people at Ann Arbor. We had regular appointments and if I was a bit anxious at these visits and felt as if I were taking "an examination," it seems I always passed with flying colors! Their delight in Elizabeth's progress gave me the deepest satisfaction. If ever I had times of fatigue and discouragement, these visits really recharged my batteries! Afterwards, it was back home again and onward and forward. Working with those friendly people was never a case of taking orders from "an expert." My husband and I were treated as equals, as parents who knew what's good for their children—and we were given the feeling that we could all learn from each other while exploring a field that was new. Together we could actually add up the world's knowledge of blind babies and pass our findings on not only to other parents like ourselves but also to the professional people who work with the blind. This seemed to add a whole other dimension to what we did.

Of all things I seemed to want most for Elizabeth it was

that she should walk. I wanted to see her on two legs, erect and independent.

Soon after she was free of the playpen and had learned to pull herself up by chair and table legs, I held her hands and we would "walk" together. But I made a point also of letting her hands brush against objects to acquaint her with her surroundings in this new standing position; and I always said the name of whatever she touched. When she could stand for a few seconds alone, I stooped down, talked or clapped my hands to encourage her to walk toward the sound.

Finally, when she was sixteen months old, Elizabeth took a few faltering steps toward me. I almost cried! I put my arms around her in a great big hug and told her she was wonderful. It was clear that she thought so too and we laughed together for joy. After each new attempt, I exclaimed "good girl." She was as pleased as we were. We never teased her by backing away to force her to take more steps, for this can be frightening, and besides is a kind of deception. For a child, trust in parents is all-important; we felt she had a right to find us where she thought we were.

Elizabeth walked independently and self-confidently when she was twenty-two months old. It happened this way.

As we were all sitting in the family room with the record player on, we suddenly noticed Elizabeth standing firmly. Presently she walked toward the music, a distance of about eight feet, without once faltering. This time, I admit, I could not control my tears.

From then on, the going was easy. She roamed freely, sometimes reverting to creeping, but walking upright more and more. When the other children left things on the floor, I continued to let them lie there, for Elizabeth must learn that there are always some obstacles in her path and find her own ways of coping. Besides, with five children, you can't keep constantly cleared up and we have settled for just picking up for company. Soon, Elizabeth seemed to develop a built-in radar system. When I thought she was about to bump into a door or chair or trip over a toy, suddenly she stopped and veered away.

Our home has a second floor and even before Elizabeth could walk, I held her hands, placed a foot on the next step until she found she must lift her legs and so could walk upward on the stairs — a new and exciting discovery. At two years, she was managing the stairs with perfect ease. When her oldest sister played records in her room, and Elizabeth downstairs, suddenly heard the music, she knew whence it came. Zoom! Off she went upstairs where she located Terri's door and called to be let in.

At first I held my breath when Elizabeth started this stair-climbing. At first too, I watched her carefully. I didn't want her to have a bad fall and be too scared to try again. And I had to gauge just what her capabilities were. I knew I must be realistic about them and yet not hover anviously when she really could manage alone. Elizabeth, too, was learning her own limitation. Even today she moves cautiously and is careful. When she was climbing on something, she used to say "she has to be careful." As I have said, she had some bumps — but no more than is par for the course with any child.

Elizabeth also had to learn not only to go up the stairs, which is relatively easy, but also how to come down by descending backward. This took time, but with help, she conquered that skill too.

The only trouble about these trips upstairs was that once she had discovered she could manage by herself, she did it more and more. I had taught her how to open dresser drawers so now she did this on her own and I would find all my belongings thrown out onto the floor. This makes for either perpetually messy or beautiful neat drawers, depending how you feel about reorganizing things at a given moment.

Climbing stairs has another advantage. After Elizabeth walked and started climbing in an upright position with me holding her hand, I always counted the steps as we went and when words started to come, she began repeating the numbers after me.

After this, it was not long before she got herself up onto the back of the couch and onto table and chairs. Pretty soon she started pulling her own little chair out of the family room and into the kitchen when I was working there, placing it close to the counter, climbing on the chair, then "helping" me mix a cake. Visitors who don't know her get very nervous watching her, but I assure them I would not allow these things unless I was as sure as it's ever possible to be, that she can do them safely.

Becoming Civilized

Watching Elizabeth learn to walk was a great pleasure for the other members of the family. But everything a child must learn to become "civilized" and live in our kind of a world is not as much fun.

Teaching Elizabeth to eat like other children was often discouraging. Make no mistake; this is a messy business even with sighted children. Nevertheless, once I was reconciled to a longer learning period and much *more* messiness, I proceeded much as I had with my others.

I bought Elizabeth her own spill-proof cup with two handles when she was six months old. I put her hands on the handles and lifted it to her mouth and tipped it so she could discover what was in it and what she must do to be able to drink it. When she could manage this with my help I took her daytime bottles away most of the time, but continued the nighttime bottle for a while longer. At ten months, she took about three ounces of milk from the cup at each of her three main meals. That seemed a fair amount, and I never tried to force more on her when she "told" me she had had enough. Like all babies, this was fun for her at first and then the cup became just another toy, and eating a game.

"Be careful, Elizabeth," I would say. "Put the glass down or you will spill the milk." Quick as a wink, she would stick her hands into the cup. Result: Spilt milk. But this is a part of learning. Elizabeth was drinking from a cup unassisted when she was about a year old. Even when she was older and had stopped spilling, I realized that she needed to feel with her hands the height of the milk in the cup so she could know how much to tip it.

As for solid foods, Elizabeth was taking baby food — fruit, meats, and cereals — when she was between six and seven months old and as I fed her, her hands were very active. Frequently she would grab the spoon, realizing that this was where her food should come from and I always encouraged this even though it slowed the meal down.

When she was nine months old, I started putting "finger foods" on her tray — bits of meat, bananas, cold cereals, toast, and best of all, chocolate chips. The chips were among the small enticing things that helped her learn to pick up small objects. At about a year, Elizabeth was eating a variety of foods and was then using both utensils and her fingers. She had scrambled eggs, bacon, potatoes and some vegetables and when I put food on her tray she searched for it and then, with her fingers, brought it to her mouth.

At first, I found that what she was really good at was throwing peas on the floor, rubbing buttered toast in her hair and eating soup with her hands (you actually can do this). But I continued getting her to grasp the spoon and then, taking her hand with the spoon in it, in *my* hand, I guided it first to the plate and then to her mouth. When she made real attempts to do this alone, I always showed my pleasure.

Even after Elizabeth could use the spoon capably, when she was around a year old, I still let her revert now and then to finger eating, feeling there was no hurry as long as she made progress. Nevertheless, the time comes when even a blind child must use utensils. It is impossible to say just when that time is. Each mother must find for herself what her child can do and find ways to make it enjoyable. Prodding and impatience only produce rebellion.

At seventeen months, Elizabeth was eating just about everything we ate and using the spoon more and more. Although at that age she had only two teeth, I discovered you don't need teeth to chew! You can gum around on ground beef, peas, chopped carrots — almost anything. Though I had read in a national magazine that blind babies must be "taught to chew" (oh, how often I have heard this!), I found this to be far from the truth. As with normal children, I gave Elizabeth bites of my baked or mashed potatoes, Jell-O, puddings, whatever was on my plate, for I had found that *if you wait too long*, children find chewing harder. All of mine progressed from baby foods to table foods, skipping the junior type.

In our home, we believe in family meals. Even when Elizabeth was a tiny baby, we brought her in her basket to the table with us when we ate so she could listen to us talk and "join in the conversation" with gurgles and squeals. Even when she was very young and I fed her most of her meal before the rest of us, I then set her in her high-chair beside us and gave her bits of whatever we had on our plates for sampling. Later, at mealtime, she sang her songs or just rattled along in her own jargon. In fact, she was our favorite floor-show and still is! Our meals are sometimes noisy, but arguing is forbidden. No one has to eat something he doesn't like or more than he wants. Forcing food on the unwilling is fatal, I find. Put the right things before children and they will take what they need. Meals are to be enjoyed.

Another messy and exasperating job for mothers is potty training. I often wonder why Nature didn't arrange to make human babies like kittens that need the minimum of "training" and seem to be born actually preferring to be what we call "clean." It's a long slow process for the human who, in infancy, sees no reason whatever for not following his own inclinations and positively enjoys messes.

When I had my first baby, seventeen years ago, I remember that the usual idea was that unless a child was toilet trained by a year old it meant you were a lazy mother. I remember sitting Terri on the pot at ten months old, not just to give her the *feel* of it, which isn't a bad idea, but actually to insist on results. For two years, I was perpetually potty-training her. It was nothing but frustration. The best way, I later found, was to observe closely and "cue in" on the readiness signs the children gave me. The time and the signs differed with each one. You have to be watchful because it is also a mistake to let the right time pass.

With Elizabeth, I realized she was likely to take even longer than any of my others because she couldn't see either the potty or what she put in it. I know too that I would have to be quite permissive about such things as feeling, touching, smelling—for here, as with all else, these senses had to substitute for vision. Some people are bothered by the primitiveness of children when it comes to these bodily necessities. I believe parents should all honestly examine their own attitudes (which often date back to their own early training) and try not to let their children grow up believing that all such things are somehow "nasty." This isn't a wholesome attitude toward the body. A person should *like* his own body — every part of it.

I have found that somewhere between 18 and 24 months is a good time to start potty training and to try a child out with training pants — then when the inevitable accident comes, tell him what he did, and take him to his potty-chair indicating that *this* is where his stools and his urine belong. I would not, however, make a big issue of these matters or punish him, or tell him it's "nasty." Often a child wants to look at his stool and examine it closely. I always permit this and am in no hurry to flush it away. I get the child himself to do this flushing in his own time so he won't think I'm arbitrarily robbing him of something he values. Though I have discouraged my older children from actually handling their stools, I feel it's natural enough at these early years for them to *want* to. With Elizabeth, however, I let her do this, and she would then sniff her hands before we washed them. How else could she learn what it's all about?

Though Elizabeth took longer than the others, her potty training followed, generally speaking, the usual pattern, —

that is, there was progress, followed by back slidings. I had found that for my older children, their very own potty chair brought more success than the small seat on the big toilet. They seemed to feel more secure. Not so, Elizabeth. She would cry pitifully and hold her urine back. I admit I was nonplussed about what to do next. The only thing I could figure out was that she thought she wasn't supposed to use her potty chair for such purposes. So for two weeks, I let it all go, only trying to make her more aware of what each of us was doing when *we* used the toilet. After her two week retreat, I again put her on her own potty — and she then used it without a whimper. But beware of thinking the job is settled once and for all; as with all children, for a long time there were relapses. One can expect that during the training process, a child will wet or have a BM only at nap or night time. This was certainly true of Elizabeth.

Nevertheless as soon as Elizabeth had become pretty reliable in the daytime, I took all her diapers off at nap time and night time too. I didn't want those diapers to be used as a crutch. I put her instead into extra thick absorbent night-panties, so if she did have an accident, she wouldn't be too soaked. This worked well, always allowing, of course for the occasional lapse.

Elizabeth was around three before I could honestly say she was mostly "trained." Perhaps it might have been sooner but I did not think it especially important though the delay made more work for mother. Yet even then, Elizabeth had not altogether accepted civilized conventions.

For instance, as I was sitting in the kitchen with a friend one day, I noticed Elizabeth sitting on her potty doing a BM. She then got up, picked up the pot and threw the contents on the floor. Though I thought I was casual about such things, this time I really jumped! Maybe that was because of my friend's presence. Then I remembered I had told Elizabeth to go to the potty herself when she needed to and this is how she carried out my suggestion! So maybe it was kind of victory in spite of the extras she added, which were all her own idea.

Sleeping

I had heard that blind babies sometimes sleep a great deal, much more than sighted children. This pattern may have to do with their inability to distinguish dark and light; but also it may be that they haven't had parents who knew the importance of constantly helping these babies discover the world outside themselves. Lacking awareness of what is around them, it is all too easy for a blind child to go on living day after day in the kind of half-world between waking up and sleeping that blindness imposes *unless* there is a special effort made to prevent it.

I made up my mind to try to establish Elizabeth's sleep routines much as I had my other children's, with allowance for whatever individual differences might be hers, just as there were also variations among my other children.

So I got her up in the mornings and down for naps at reasonable hours with her "blanky," her musical Santa Claus and Jingle Bells. And soon she learned to go fast asleep. When it seemed to me that she had slept enough, I waked her gently, talked and played with her a bit before actually taking her from her crib. Above all, I tried to make her waking hours so full of interesting discoveries and fascinating things to do that she never had time to be bored. I had observed plenty of grownups, too, tend to "withdraw into sleep" when they are bored and yet are wide awake as soon as something stimulating comes along.

So, as with my other children, I put Elizabeth to bed at regular times and soon she seemed to develop her own inner clock. I suspect some mothers mistakenly conclude that if their blind child sleeps a great deal, it is because he has a special need for it. But I can't help suspecting that the mother may be secretly relieved to have a difficult child out of the way.

Eye Pressing

So called "bad habits" I handled much as I had with the other children. I tried not to punish, bribe, nag, threaten or scold. I found something else for them to do that was more interesting and joined in the fun of whatever it was.

Nevertheless, I learned that blind children have some unpleasant habits and mannerisms that are characteristic and are known as "blindisms." One of these is eye pressing. They put both hands on their eyes and press, sometimes hard and long. No one has a final explanation for this. It may be that it relieves some discomfort in blind eyes. It may be that the pressing produces bright flashes which are fun to make come and go. It does not, I am told, cause the eyes to get pressed deep into the socket as I had first believed. Blind eyes often recede and take on that deep-set look because the non-functioning eye tends to dry out and get smaller, and so occupies less of the socket than the normal eye.

But eye-pressing is an unattractive habit and tends to mark a child as peculiar; so we always discourage it when we can. When Elizabeth puts her hands to her eyes we say "no" and very gently remove the hands and give her something else to do. We never speak sternly or jerk her. Just as with other "bad habits" which children fall into, Elizabeth presses her eyes most when she is tired or cross or for some reason under tension. If this seems to be so, I cuddle her or rock her on my lap or sing to her, or perhaps carry her off to bed a bit earlier than usual. If that is not the case, then an interesting substitute occupation is likely to do the trick.

I am not trying to make this sound easier than it is. With Elizabeth, the need to press her eyes seemed for a long time to run in streaks. For months at a time, she would scarcely ever do this. Then for a straight week she would have her hands to her eyes a great deal of the time.

Now the habit has receded. Today, Elizabeth rarely presses her eyes; and when she does, usually complies without getting cross when I say, "Take your hands down, Elizabeth." Then I find something else which is irresistible to occupy those hands.

All this calls for patience and resourcefulness in parents. That is true with all children; but more of both is required with a blind child.

Talking, Singing

Elizabeth has talked for so long that it is hard for me to remember when it started.

Children learn to talk by being talked to. Fortunately, most mothers babble away to their babies long before they can understand — and hearing these sounds lays the groundwork for later speech. When parents are the silent type and find it hard to talk to their infants, it usually takes them longer to learn. Elizabeth and I had no earth-shaking conversations in the first months but I did make a point of talking to her even more than with my other children.

At bath-time for instance, when I splashed the water at her I said I was splashing water. The other children loved to see her in the tub and we encouraged her to turn the faucet on and let the water run over her hands; we showed her how to rub soap on the washcloth. We called by name everything she did. We also called by name all the parts of her body and let her feel them. Like so many children she especially loved her belly button. When the bath was finally over we urged her to lift the drain and listen to the water go gurgling out, all the time telling her what was happening.

Whenever she picked something up, we would tell her what it was and how it worked. And we laughed and sang and exclaimed. Words! Words! The names of things and acts. You sit, stand, jump. There is a sink, a faucet, water. Water is wet, ice is cold, the stove is hot. When you want a drink, you are thirsty.

And so Elizabeth began to make all sorts of sounds too — just for fun at first and then, between ten and eleven months, she began to make sounds which, if not exactly words, at least meant something definite to her — a special sound for getting ready to eat, for example — and another for certain games we played.

The people in her world were especially important. At a little past a year old, she began to try to say "Terri" in imitation of my saying it — or "daddy." At about this time too, she was trying out a lot of "ga's," "wa's," and "da's" and so making more and more of the various sounds in the English language. By a year and a half she could intelligibly repeat words with various inflections and intent.

Very shortly, came imitative phrases like "oh dear" and like all children, she responded to practiced questions like, "What does the kitty-cat say?" with a hearty "meow."

At a year and eight months she began to volunteer "good night" at bedtime and to use expressions like "leave alone" or "drink milk."

Not until she was past two did she begin to use negatives. "Elizabeth *no* tired — *no* bed," etc.

How did she learn that a chair was a chair and not a couch?

At first she did call the couch a chair. So I got her to walk the length of the couch with her hand on it while I said "Couch." "The couch is long." and then, as she ran her hand over the chair, "The chair is short."

I started teaching Elizabeth her ABC's when she was about a year and a half. I knew it all meant absolutely nothing to her; but it gave her a chance to practice them and discover that the grownups were pleased. She can discover later what letters are for.

Of course Elizabeth for a long time confused the personal pronouns. When hungry, she said "You hungry, you want to eat," echoing the words I had said to her. She was three when she first began to use them properly, for this is a rather difficult matter to grasp and it was only gradually that she got the idea. At this age, we made no effort to correct her, confident that as she developed and heard the proper use around her, she would catch on. But even now, when she is approaching five; she may say "her" for "I," but only when under some emotional stress.

We are a singing family. I believe this has been very important for Elizabeth's ability to "vocalize," for songs introduce children not only to many new words and their sounds but also to melody.

There are two recording artists who made a record together and as the record plays, Elizabeth sings along with them. It is a very moving thing to hear that child singing along with them, every word, every note perfect; I have seen tears in the eyes of friends who know Elizabeth when they hear her singing along with the record.

One of the songs that is a favorite with Elizabeth is "He's Got the Whole World in His Hands." She has sung it including each member of the family by name — Terri, Sharon, Mommie, etc. Recently she has added some of her friends from the Project at Ann Arbor.

Music is one of this child's greatest joys in life. I can only pray it will remain so. But we have also acquired storytelling records such as "The Elephant's Child," "I Hear a Sound," "To Lick a Pickle." There are also records that describe and illustrate various musical instruments. They can be bought at many grocery stores and supermarkets and I would advise parents whether their children are blind or sighted to acquire a store of them.

So we have surrounded her with music. As well as a record player, we have an electric organ and a small chord organ for a child which we keep in the family room. Elizabeth can turn it on and play with it as the fancy hits her. And how she sings! Her little voice is constantly lifted in song. She joins the older children in singing along with their records and seems to know hundreds — Girl Scout songs, Romper Room songs, Beatles and Monkees records and many others. Among the first words that Elizabeth put together were "record on, record on." Today, when she isn't talking, she can be heard singing to herself. She has an excellent ear and if I make a mistake or sing off key she is right there to correct me with both words and tune.

As soon as it seemed sensible, we started taking Elizabeth to church with us and she soon knew the Mass better than some older children. When it comes to the great "Amen" as it is sung three times in three different octaves, she joins in eagerly even, sometimes, keeping on after everyone else has stopped. But nobody minds.

I have to admit she isn't always perfectly behaved on these occasions but people know her and are tolerant. One day I wanted her to stop fooling around on the kneeling benches and kept tugging at her. Presently her voice could be heard saying loudly, "Oh damn! Leave her alone!" Such moments of embarrassment seem to us a small price to pay for having her with us in church where she hears the voices and music.

I take her up in the organ loft sometimes and one day, one of the choir members asked Elizabeth why she had not joined in a certain song. Quick as a wink Elizabeth said, "I hate that song!" So it is clear that she has strong preferences and no hesitation about expressing them.

Elizabeth and Her Family

Elizabeth's brothers and sisters have contributed immeasurably to her growth and happiness and she, in turn, has taught them compassion, patience, and love.

"Ma, quick! Watch Elizabeth give me a kiss."

"One thing, Ma, if you ever have another blind baby you will have had experience."

"Ma, have I had Elizabeth outside long enough?"

Yes, they have done more for her than her father and I could have ever done by ourselves. They treat her as one of them. They have helped her discover the world outdoors better than we could because they see it with the eyes of children. They lug her around to inspect trees, grass, stones, flowers, dogs, cats and to listen to the birds that sing. With her, they sample the new tricycle, try the swing, the sandbox, the wading pool and get her acquainted with the neighbor's children.

I believe it is of great importance that a mother of any handicapped child should never let that child take so much of her time or so absorb her emotionally that she loses her awareness of her other children's needs or her husband's.

Each child is a unique human being and should be individually considered. If you have five children, it is likely that you must develop five different approaches to them, yet with equal concern for each. Though your husband is your partner in all that you do, he also has the right to find that you are fully his wife as well as the mother of his children.

In some ways of course, Elizabeth is bound to be "special." She takes more of my time, more conscious planning for and "teaching." Yet one of the important things she must learn is to fit into a family and to understand that there are others all around her who have desires and rights. So as soon as she seemed able to get the idea, at around the age of three, I made a point of not letting her impose on the others and urged my other children to stick up for themselves when she interfered, as indeed, like all children, she often did. I am still teaching her to wait her turn, not to interrupt whoever is talking and not to grab some fascinating toy until her turn comes. I know from experience how hard this is and that it is perhaps never mastered perfectly. But Elizabeth must learn this along with the rest — and we must all help.

As I write Terri (Terese) my first-born little girl is seventeen and about to graduate from high school. Time passes so quickly. I remember so vividly, holding her in my arms and cuddling her when she was first born and thinking it was all too good to be true. I was a *mother!* Her father sent me a dozen red roses then and has done this with each of my babies. What a thrill that gave me, and still does whenever I think about it!

Today Terri is an attractive young lady, every inch a teenager — on the one hand, a bit shy and stiff and yet, at times voluble and talkative. Although she can be moody and self-absorbed, when the chips are down, one discovers she is idealistic and responsible. She writes poetry and paints a little and these both have a touch of sadness in them.

Like many adolescents Terri is concerned about her appearance, has had her hair "frosted." In front of the mirror, she turns this way and that to see if her figure is stylishly thin and examines her skin for blemishes. At times she finds the whole family very trying and her brothers and sisters "creeps," sent to torment her. She just can't wait to get away from home and be rid of us all, she says. Yet as a child, she couldn't bear to spend the night at a friend's house across the street and declared she would get sick if she did. I believe she is inwardly fighting her dependence on her home and that getting away to Junior College soon will help her find herself.

Whenever she has time, she works at a local eating place, having overcome her shyness enough to go and present herself for a job. She gets a dollar an hour plus those tips that add much to her income. All this gives her a good feeling.

She has expressed a desire to work some day with handicapped children, "but not blind children," she adds. The teacher training course she will take at college is bound to be good preparation for whatever future choice she mades in that field. We are proud of this young lady.

Next comes Mark, our black-haired, tanned-skin fifteen-year-old. He is a worrier. He worries if he doesn't understand what his teacher says in school. He worries if he can't get his hair cut on a certain day. He is our "why" boy. At four, he had to know just how his bike worked; now his "whys" are about such things as war and race prejudice. He has, I think, a gift for a sensitive awareness of personal relations. He is the one who comes and gives me a kiss when I least expect it. When his father and I kiss, he smiles and says, "You and Dad really love each other, don't you?"

Next in age is Sherri, my little namesake, now thirteen. She is small like me with black hair and fair skin. She is the least argumentative of my children, makes friends easily and brings a kind of spark into the room when she comes, as well as being the peacemaker in the family. She plays the guitar and organ all by ear. For her, life is usually busy and happy. If she isn't drawing or baking cookies, she may be down the street at a neighbor's house learning to make an apron. She has always been a child to make your heart sing and pleasantly uncomplicated, until rather recently.

Just now, both Mark and Sherri are typical teen-agers exhibiting the usual highs and lows of adolescence, each in his way. Either they are calm and reasonable or hysterically unreasonable. They will talk a leg off you or, at another time, enter the land of complete silence. Pressed for an answer to a question when they are in one of these "I-don't-belong-any-where-in-the-world" moods, you're lucky if you get a grunt from them.

It balances out, though. After one of Mark's bad moods, I returned home one day, to find he had not only picked up his clothes but vacuumed the house — a gift much appreciated especially as I had never asked him to. And Sherri sometimes leaves a love-note on my bed stand to atone for a day of difficulties.

As for Dickie, everyone should have a Dickie. There is something especially dear about him. He is the one who crawls into bed with me and we talk and talk. It may be about little Amy who kisses him in school or why it was that he lost his mittens or tore his pants. It's always "nobody's" fault. Once he asked how grown men made money to feed their families and he guessed he wouldn't want to work when he grew up. The trouble is, I half believe him.

He has had some so-called "problems" in school and it was thought best to keep him in kindergarten an extra year. So at seven, he was still in the first grade. That year he just lagged along for a while, in his happy-go-lucky way, seemingly uninterested in working — then, in the second half of the school term he began to pick up. He was given all sorts of tests, besides an eye examination (normal). To make a long story short, I had a talk with the principal who assured me that Dickie was "above average" in intelligence and that any trouble was "developmental." Nevertheless, I knew that people at the school and elsewhere had all been wondering whether because of Elizabeth's special demands on me, Dickie had been neglected when he was still hardly more than a baby. I honestly don't think so and it's hard for me to know that this suspicion is in people's minds. Besides, Dickie is not the kind of child you can "neglect"! He has a way of making himself felt. If he feels like love, he wraps himself around you; and if he is angry, he expresses himself in no uncertain terms. If I won't let him do something he wants to do, he will holler at me, "I don't like you any more!"

Once, when I was cuddling Elizabeth, Dickie was watching me and said, "Do you love Elizabeth more than me?" I replied, "Come here, Dickie" and, putting my arms around him said, "Every Mommy loves *all* her children. It doesn't matter if you have twelve. And I love you a bushel and a peck and a hug around your neck." Then I gave him a big kiss.

Now, at eight, Dickie has nearly made up for lost time and soon will be entering the third grade and he is going strong. It has been a great growing year for him — both mentally and physically. Also, he made his first Holy Communion — and what a moving sight that was for all of us!

I made up a good night song for all my children, and Elizabeth and sometimes Dickie still want me to sing it to them when I tuck them into bed. The others have outgrown this. But of all my children, I seem to feel that it's still Terri and Mark who most need occasional signs of affection even if they appear not to care. In a way, they make it a bit hard to "love" them but I know it's important not to let this get lost in the hustle and bustle of daily life. Giving close attention to the things that interest them means a great deal to them and the tone of voice used in talking with them conveys more than the words.

Because I know that many people have wondered what effect Elizabeth's blindness had on my other children, whether it made them feel embarrassed or made us seem "different" from other families, I decided one day recently to ask each one. I am well aware that asking children a straight question does not always bring out a true answer. All of us use words to cover up as well as to reveal feelings, especially when we don't like to admit them even to ourselves. But for what they're worth, here are their answers:

Terri: She seemed reluctant at first to answer and I told

her she didn't have to if she didn't want to. Then she said, "She's blind, you can't do anything about it. How am I supposed to feel? If anybody at school asked me about her, I used to practically start crying, but that's past. I love her very much. One time, I wished she had never been born but that wasn't because she was blind. I wanted to get a suntan and instead I had to stay in and watch her." (We used to give Terri five dollars a week to help me with Elizabeth and watch her when I had to be busy elsewhere.)

I told Terri I understood how she must have felt because I could see she felt badly about saying this. I told her that even mothers — even "good mothers" — when they are tired or discouraged wish at these times that they could lie back and think only of themselves.

Mark:

"When we first knew Elizabeth was blind, I was scared and wondered what she would be like, how she would do things. I was sad when I looked into her eyes. At first I was afraid she might hurt herself. Now I like her because everybody asks about her and what we do together."

Sherri:

"I wondered what she was going to be like. I thought maybe she couldn't play like other children. Now I think of her as if she could see because she acts that way. She is an angel and I don't know what I would do without her."

Dickie:

(He could hardly wait for his turn to answer my question though he was so young when Elizabeth was born that he can't remember a great deal.)

"It seems like she can see. She can't ride a bike. I love her and wish she wasn't blind."

All the children treat Elizabeth differently than they do each other. They are never sharp or cross with her and if Elizabeth takes advantage of any one of them, I have to be the one to step in. I've never made them feel that they must sacrifice themselves to Elizabeth or let her become a burden.

I am convinced that in most things children take their

cues from their parents. If I had let myself be a slave to Elizabeth and acted martyred I'm sure they would have caught this attitude and felt resentful. But I insist on having a life of my own too — with my husband, with my friends and the many things I do in the community.

My own family is large and at family get-togethers like Christmas, Elizabeth is with cousins by the dozen. But I have to watch her. A great deal of noise and confusion befuddles her and when it gets too much for her, she holds her hands over her ears and begs to go home. She still can't stand all the attention that her relatives tend to lavish on her and I have made it plain to relatives and friends alike that if she shows she doesn't want to be handled, to leave her alone. This has paid off and now she is becoming increasingly friendly to strangers if they will let her take time and aren't noisy or over-demonstrative.

II

At Three:
The World Is Her Oyster

At this time Elizabeth was developing so fast on all fronts that
it has been hard to trace the exact moments of her new accomplishments. We have all been interested in the kinds of play
she has enjoyed, in the changes from simple to relatively
complex.

She has never been a great doll girl, preferring to move
about and explore new places, playing with small objects such
as dice, checkers, poker chips, and taking them in and out of
bags or cups. At about this age she did lots of "pretending."
She held walnuts to her ears, calling them "earrings," put a
bowl on her head for a "hat," teased me by calling her milk
"coffee." Once, she took some excelsior from a box and spread it
over her head, saying it was a "wig." (I have one for special
occasions and had let her feel it while telling her what it is
for.)

As soon as I could I drew Elizabeth into my own activities
as much as possible and encouraged her to "help" me. When
I cleaned windows, I gave her a cloth and showed her how
she too could clean. I got her to clean her own small chair.
I let her lick the cake batter and icing when I mixed them.
I even asked her to help mop the floor, giving her a small
pail and cloth, and starting her at one end of the kitchen
while I worked from the other.

She continued to explore the kitchen cupboards, learning
to find the various pots and pans and call them by name. I

let her open the refrigerator and identify what was there by both touch and smell. In the kitchen, she especially enjoyed sitting in the double sink, swinging the faucet around and giving herself a bath. I was careful about the hot water and even now I don't depend on her knowing how to be sure she turns on only the cold.

We also worked at this time on removing the plastic covering on individually wrapped slices of cheese, a hard operation for anyone but excellent exercise for fine finger coordination.

Blocks have been part of Elizabeth's standard toy equipment for a long time and I had gone through the ritual of stacking them and letting her feel how a block tower can grow. Quite suddenly, or so it seemed, she got the idea and surprised me when she was three and a half by spending almost a whole day building and, of course, crying bitterly when the whole thing toppled and fell. So I worked with her on how to stack the blocks evenly and explained also that there is such a thing as *too* high when the tower will inevitably collapse.

At this time Elizabeth could not yet dress herself but we worked on this and soon she could perform some of the simpler operations if we focused on whatever was most fun to do.

She has been bouncing on beds since she was ten months old and, like all children, adores this. At first, of course, I held her hands but around three, she could do it safely by herself. Visitors watching this were invariably alarmed, wondering if she knew where the edges of the bed were and fearing a bad fall. I could assure them that Elizabeth knew every nook and cranny of this house, including the beds and their limits, and that she was quite dependable.

Though there is much to learn and to do in one's home, it is important to get any child, including a blind child, out into an ever widening world.

When Elizabeth was just short of three, her sister Sharon was asked to give a report in school on anything she liked and asked us if she might describe what we did to bring Elizabeth up to be a normal child. We agreed that she should show the class a Braille book I had, entitled "Sounds We Hear," so the children could get an idea of how blind children eventually can learn to read. She was to show also the toys we use and how they are chosen for sound, texture, smell and so on. Then the teacher asked if I would be willing to bring Elizabeth herself to school so the children could actually see her. I had already taken her to Dickie's kindergarten class where she had a gay time, and we gladly consented. I hoped, too, that the children would see that Elizabeth was not much different from them and so help overcome that "shying away" reaction which I have already described as so common among people in the presence of what seems to them "abnormal."

So off we went, and the schoolchildren, sixty of them, not to mention the teacher who seemed to be just as curious as they, had the experience of concentrating for quite a time on a small blind child. They all said, "Hi, Elizabeth," and laughed at her antics and she laughed happily back. Then I volunteered to answer questions. They wanted to know: "Does she see nothing but black?" "Can she read the Braille book?" "Does she have teeth?" "Will she ever be able to play baseball?" and, from the teacher, "Do you have to watch her all the time?" and "Can she feed herself with a spoon?" I explained how many of these things took time and how I went about it, and I felt I had accomplished my mission of showing these children that although it takes extra patience and though some things like baseball, for example, Elizabeth would always have to forego, she would eventually be able to get along much like any other child. I demonstrated her toys, too, and explained how Elizabeth's "Touch and Learn" book with various shapes and textures to trace and feel, would help her develop "educated hands" and so prepare her for learning Braille someday.

By this time, I was taking Elizabeth on trips with me whenever possible. She went along when the other children had a dentist appointment for example, making friends with the dentist and people in the waiting room.

She loved especially to wander around the grocery store feeling everything and grabbing her favorites. She could by then locate the gumball machine and was learning that it takes a penny to get one. She recognized the milk, meat, vegetable and bread counters. She would pick up a box and say, "There's cookies" and put it into the basket though it wasn't always cookies. She might take a box of chocolates, smell it, tell me what it was and add it to our purchases. The people who run the store knew her well and were glad to let her forage this way.

Across the street from our house is a large and pleasant restaurant, and sometimes we took Elizabeth there to eat. She loved to go, swinging happily along with one hand in mine and the other in her father's as we walked the short distance. She would say, "Go out to eat at the Red Brick." When the waitress came to take our order, she would say, "Fry frenchies, Jell-O, milk." She felt the milk carefully, then lifted the glass in two hands. After she ate, she would get down from the high chair and wander cheerfully about among the guests who greeted her with smiles. The owner knows us and so do the waitresses but many of the guests were strangers and, I believe, did not suspect that she was blind. She still goes with us to the Red Brick and we watch her as she moves about but we do not leave the table to follow her.

We now started letting Elizabeth out to play alone in the sandbox in the back yard where I could keep an eye on her. She wandered around the grounds slowly and carefully so I did not fear for her there. She would feel out the whole back of the house; get into the window wells. She soon located the screen porch and where the latch is so she could let herself in. But one day the door was latched from the inside. This presented a real problem and I watched her go to work on it, her small hands feeling out the possibilities. Finally she located a break in the screening, the result of a fast baseball game. She examined it, then began working her way through it — a tight squeeze. Half way through, she felt the cement flooring of the porch which told her she was where she wanted to be. She backed up, then made the big plunge, went on through the opening and reached her goal.

At Three: the World Is Her Oyster

We gave Elizabeth a wading pool and tried to show her that it was fun to get into the water as well as just splashing with her hands while sitting outside. I got in, Terri got in and we made a big thing of how great it was. No go. Elizabeth cried if we tried to put her in so we gave up. I drained the pool and put it on the porch. Later that day we were surprised to find Elizabeth standing beside it and feeling the whole inside of it. No water. Then she got in and scooted all around the empty pool and played that way for an hour. The next day there was a dramatic change. Having decided for herself how big it was and just what it was like, when it had passed the "Elizabeth test" — as it were — she then got into it when it was full of water and thoroughly enjoyed herself.

My friend Betty has seven children and a swimming pool! This home swarms with kids and Elizabeth dearly loves to go there. In the house, there are three steps leading from Betty's family room to the kitchen and Elizabeth had to learn to negotiate these. At first, all the children clustered around to see that she didn't fall and Elizabeth became very perturbed. Then she said in a peremptory tone of voice, "Just leave her alone!"

Betty laughed and said, "That's spunk for you." And indeed she has plenty of just that and is learning to hold her own with others. But she also must accommodate.

It is a real temptation to give her too much help. I described how, very early, I encouraged her to listen to where something fell and then to feel around for it and this must be continued. I have always encouraged her to listen to where something falls and then to feel around for it. Usually she accepts the job of hunting, but sometimes she's just not in the mood. I sometimes have to prevent my other children from being her willing slaves. I remember when she dropped a whole box of checkers which rolled hither and yon while all the children scurried to pick them up, whereupon she dropped them all again — clearly on purpose — and yelled, "Dickie, Terri, pick up her checkers!" I told her she had dropped them and she must pick them up. "Or not!" screamed Elizabeth, which means "no." Then she picked up a few and flung them all around again, mad as a hornet. I leaned over and gave her three smacks on her bottom, the non-hurting kind — but she got the message. It took her a while to calm down but soon she was her old self. When she started to retrieve the checkers, we all gave her *some* help — and she has not tried that trick again. Such experiences are part of learning to be self sustaining; it begins in the family and goes on into widening circles.

III

Willingly to School

The next step: How to provide for my little girl's on-going?

In the back of my mind for a long time had been the vision of her in nursery school, taking her place among children her own age enjoying many new experiences and achieving the beginnings of doing without home and mother.

It seemed to me that she was now *ready* — not just because she was nearly four, but because of her self possession and signs of inner security. She had lived her life in a loving home and I had confidence that the basic trust this gave her would now carry over into the wider world.

How does one choose a nursery school? What should one look for?

The most important thing, I believe, is the kind of person the teacher is. Although she needs knowledge of how children grow and learn and what it is fair to expect of them at varying ages, she should also have a relaxed and happy approach to them. Her job requires an innate sensitivity to their individual differences and the knack of developing the best in each.

One should observe also the physical surroundings. Is there adequate space both indoors and out? There should be creative playthings — the kind that can be used in many different ways—and equipment that calls for the use of a child's whole body as well as his hands. Sometimes space is so cramped and equipment so meager that one can do better at home.

There should be sensible health supervision. This includes alertness to signs of a beginning cold or fever and provision for isolating a child who may be developing an illness contagious to the others until someone can come and take him home.

I would put high on my list too, the importance of a friendly approach to parents as well as children — a willingness on the teacher's part to seize an occasional moment for an exchange of thoughts about happenings in a child's life at home which may affect his behavior in school—and vice versa. Teachers and parents should be partners. Each knows the child from a different standpoint and so can contribute to the other's understanding.

In my small Michigan town there were not many choices; but one day a miracle happened, my luck was holding.

When Elizabeth was just past three and a half, I noticed two blocks from my home, in front of what had once been a small school-house, but long in disuse, a sign saying, SUNNY CORNERS NURSERY SCHOOL — OPENING SOON. There was a telephone number which I quickly jotted down and when I got home, I lost no time in calling it. I said I wanted to come and talk about enrolling my three and a half year old daughter. Alas! Though the answering voice was a pleasant one, I was told that only children who had passed their fourth birthday could be accepted. This seemed a big setback until "the voice" finally said that there might, later on, during the summer months, be a class taking younger children too.

This actually came to pass. A while later the lady owner of the nice voice, who is now my good friend Pat, called and asked me to come to see her and bring Elizabeth who would be nearly four when the class started.

"Fine," I said, and then, for the first time mentioned that my child was blind.

Silence at the other end. Then came some halting words about not being sure she could manage, there was the "effect on the other children"; she herself had never "worked with the handicapped," and so on. I replied that Elizabeth was an altogether normal little girl and that I would be willing to come to school and stay as long as needed to show how a blind child

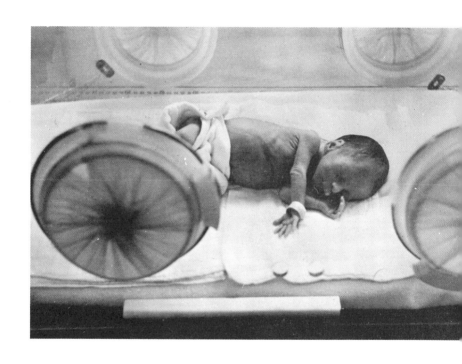

Elizabeth at birth

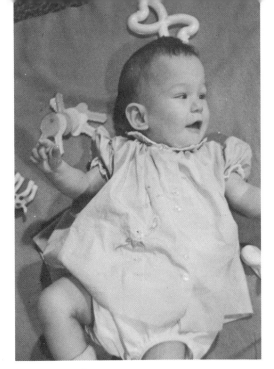

At six months

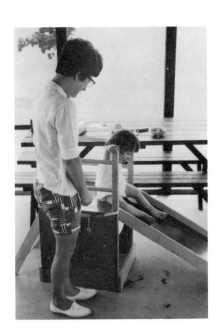

Mrs. Ulrich
and Elizabeth
(at eighteen months)

Elizabeth with her sister, Terri

Two years old

Potty training

Elizabeth at nursery school

Elizabeth at nursery school

At four and a half years

April, 1970. Mrs. Ulrich and Elizabeth

could participate and fit into a group of normal children. I added that Elizabeth had already been much among other children her age, that they paid little attention to the fact that she was blind but accepted her as one of them.

It was a great tribute to Pat's flexibility, one of her priceless assets, that she soon saw this situation as a challenge rather than as a hopeless obstacle. It seemed as though I could almost hear her unspoken ponderings, of the pros and cons. Then she asked me to bring Elizabeth to see her.

So Elizabeth and I visited the school which was now almost ready to start and it did not take Pat long to become intrigued with that little girl and to realize that she was not only quite competent but might also provide a valuable experience for the other children. She observed that Elizabeth's speech was clear, her vocabulary well developed, that she walked with confidence. She discovered her lovely responsiveness. Then, like so many others, she said, "She doesn't seem blind."

I believe that my offer to come for as long as needed clinched matters. I had meant my services to be temporary and only later discovered I had talked myself right into a job at a moment in my life when I had no help at home. And it proved to be true that Elizabeth at first needed more help than the other children and it was hardly fair to expect Pat to learn in a week or so what had taken me four years — just how to go about making constant use of all Elizabeth's senses and always remembering that "her hands are her eyes."

I knew that the school delighted me and that it was what I wanted for Elizabeth as her next big step forward. There was a cheery note about the place. Although my little girl could never see the walls painted in soft colors, the flower murals or the pots of flowers outdoors — these all spoke to me of a happy approach to a child's day that Elizabeth would be bound to feel. And I knew she could enjoy the outdoor equipment.

In the yard, there was a slide, see-saws, a whirl-a-gig and different-sized rubber tires anchored upright for children to climb in and out. Indoors, there were two large rooms with a piano in one for Pat to play for the children's marching or singing. There was certainly a wealth of play materials — a basketball hoop swinging from a steel beam over which the children could drape themselves and go spinning around or use in any other way they found fun. There was a kitchen corner for real cooking; a doll corner, a blackboard. There were plenty of small sturdy chairs and tables, a tent, a punching bag, blocks of all shapes and sizes. These were immediately visible but, as I soon learned, much was stored also on shelves and in boxes until needed. Here could be found puzzles, painting materials, scissors and paste, and beads to string, all so important for Elizabeth in the further training of those hands.

So Elizabeth was enrolled for the summer session with me in attendance, too; and when fall came, we agreed that I should stay on as general assistant in return for tuition. School was to be in session two days a week from nine until twelve.

"Oh, well," I thought, "I'll just cut corners with my housework on school days." My other children would be in school for big slices of time and anyway, they were old enough to take real responsibility for certain household chores. I went home and put it to them this way. Did they agree that it would be a big thing for Elizabeth to have this chance to be with children who would treat her as an equal and help prevent her getting the idea that she was different and special? This led to quite a discussion but in the end they agreed.

I was disappointed, to be sure, that Elizabeth was to have her mother on hand at all times. I was especially eager for her to learn without me once she felt at home with these strange children, with Pat and with the lay-out of Sunny Corners. But to some extent, we found our way around this. After she had settled down, we arranged for me to absent myself occasionally for short times. I would say to Elizabeth, "Mother has to run home for a minute. I'll be back very soon and Pat will be right here if you need something."

By now, I was pretty sure that Elizabeth had discovered that mothers do come back when they say they will. Even in those earlier days when she was most dependent on me and would carry on and cry bitterly when I left her, I never fooled her by sneaking out of the house when she wasn't looking. I told her that I was going and kept my word about when I'd be back. If I had to be away longer than planned, I talked to her on the phone. I always explained carefully who would be there to take care of her while I was away and I set up some interesting play for her. To make my going more bearable, I would promise a small gift when I returned.

So, at school, when I said I was leaving, she would answer "Bye, Mom," and when I returned and called to her, "Here I am, Elizabeth," she greeted me happily, grasped me around the waist for a quick hug, and hurried back to her job.

I don't want to pretend that everything was perfect. There were occasional rough moments such as the problems of jealousy at having to share me with others, for of course I was there for all the children, not just for Elizabeth. When another child crawled into my lap or pushed Elizabeth aside when I was with her, she resented it, returning push for push and screaming at the intruder. What I then did was to take both on my lap for a quick hug and kiss all around and then get them quickly back to business. Often this worked, but there were some bad moments too.

There were also some real concessions that had to be made to Elizabeth's blindness, but mostly these were minor things that Pat and I could work out. For instance, when the children were pasting, I would put a small dab of paste on a piece of paper for Elizabeth and guide her hand to locate it. This prevented her tangling with the others when they reached for a communal paste pot.

When marching time came, I at first took Elizabeth's hand and guided her. But she soon got the idea about as well as the others, for they all tended to wander all over, instead of staying in line. Naturally, she bumped into things sometimes but so did many of the children and I had to call Pat's attention to the fact that Elizabeth's small mishaps were often no more than all children have. Yet once Pat got the idea that

Elizabeth was pretty competent, she actually did forget sometimes that she was blind and so occasionally missed her cue.

The first day of school I remember, Pat held out a cookie to Elizabeth who thereupon did nothing. Then I said, "Elizabeth, Pat has a cookie for you." Up shot her hand, Pat placed the cookie in it and Elizabeth devoured it with a broad grin.

After school had been in session for awhile, one of the children got a box of playdough from a shelf and Elizabeth immediately demanded playdough too. Amazed, Pat turned to me wonderingly and asked however Elizabeth knew what it was. It was the smell, of course. Playdough has a very distinctive smell which Elizabeth recognized at once for she had long known it.

All that I did to help Elizabeth had for a long time become second nature to me; Pat had to observe how constantly I managed to get Elizabeth to feel, smell, taste and hear things; how I described carefully where something was, or got her to feel my hand when I was doing something. I would tell Elizabeth that the cookie was on the table near the pitcher which she had already located; or I let her feel my hands when I pared an apple. These are things that sighted children learn by seeing. But since with blind children, the knowledge must come through the other senses, a teacher of the blind has to acquire such habits.

Pat was a quick learner and before long, Elizabeth needed only a little more attention than the others and Pat could give it as well as I could. Then I only helped Elizabeth when she happened to be near me and left as much as possible to Pat, for after all, what I most wanted was for this child to learn to do without me as much as possible. Pat was the teacher, I was just the Mama. And Elizabeth along with the other children, must know this.

When school started in the morning, the children took their places in chairs and, when assembled, we usually played the game, "getting ready to go to school." With hands and fingers we simulated brushing hair and teeth and putting on clothes. Sometimes we got toothpaste on noses and had to wash it off; we might decide to gargle with water. We pretended a quick breakfast, then got into the car, turning the key to the starter and so on. When on the road, we might encounter some surprise obstacles like turtles or toads and then we would slow down carefully, draw up at the side of the road and after looking up and down the road, get out and remove the small animal from harm's way. Sometimes it was a cow that had strayed in front of us and in this case, we just honked loudly. This was great fun for the children who all made tremendous honking sounds which they were very unwilling to stop.

Some of this was new to Elizabeth so at first I guided her hands through the motions. When we were *actually* in our car and leaving home for school, I let Elizabeth feel the ignition key and called her attention to what it felt like to slow down and pull over.

After this game, the children would scatter to find a job that interested them. Some were quite positive about what they wanted to do, others needed suggestions. At this time, Pat and I worked with each child individually for a short time, perhaps helping him learn to tie shoes, print his name, recognize numbers and letters, distinguish between right and left hand. Children develop these skills at very differing speeds, but at school they all made at least a beginning. We found also that each child seemed to relish having a time all to himself with either Pat or me and sometimes wanted a little hug along with the teaching. We never interrupted a child who seemed oblivious of us, engrossed in what he was doing.

Next came a period of marching to music—or we played various games that involved rhythm. Then the children seemed ready to settle down to some group "teaching" to prepare them for someday learning to read. This reading readiness period involved reviewing the recognition of letters and numbers which we had first worked on with them individually. They also looked at large posters on which were pictured various objects, the names of which sounded alike with the exception of one that was different. "Which is it?" we asked. For instance, "hat," "cat," "bat," "mat," "*dog*." This works well in a group, for the children who are less sure catch on as they listen to the others.

The attention span of children this age, although it varies with each child and depends too on how great his interest is in a special task, is quite limited. Especially during this teaching period, we watched carefully for signs of wandering attention and we never pressed a child beyond his limits, even if he had not yet grasped what we were trying to make clear. We let him turn to something else. But we believed he should never feel displeasure from us or get the feeling that he was failing. No matter what — we tried to build self-confidence, enjoyment and a sense of success in the mastery of a new skill.

Though Elizabeth could not participate in those parts of learning that depend specifically on vision, there was much she could do with the many materials and activities that she had already encountered at home before her school days.

For instance, there were what I called "messy projects." We made our own "clay" with flour, salt, water and food coloring. We dumped all those into a bowl and the children then mixed the concoction with their hands. They loved this, and Elizabeth especially wanted to keep on pushing and squeezing it through her fingers before finally molding it into some shape.

We finger painted too, dipping hands into a jar of paint made for just this purpose, then smearing it any way at all over a large sheet of paper. This results in an abstract art effect which is sometimes quite beautiful. We painted also with regular paint and brushes but very freely. The painting need not represent anything unless the child himself said so. We let fancy roam.

For pure fun, we used to get one of the children to lie down on a large piece of paper while another traced his outline and so produced a "portrait." Each wanted to be the one to lie down but had to wait his turn, which was good practice for them. Afterwards, each was allowed to take his own portrait home.

We always had snack time. Children need a bit of nourishment and a change of pace during a busy morning. They had

Koolaid or milk and cookies and Pat and I had a real coffee break, for which we were very ready.

We did real cooking too. The children helped make a mix for cookies or produced a Jell-O dessert. They helped set the table. Once we had a pancake breakfast for parents first thing in the morning when they brought the kids. Then, as well as helping mix the batter, the children got a chance to try flipping the pancake over — not an easy operation.

Marshmallows had many uses. We made snowmen of them, with toothpick arms and legs and whole cloves stuck in for features. We could glue these to a cereal box with the front cut out and bits of cotton pasted on the back for a snow storm. All sorts of simple materials were made to serve in many ingenious ways — bottle caps, yarn, raw peas to paste in various patterns on colored paper, bright sequins, colored kernels of popcorn.

We went outdoors whenever weather permitted and it was amusing to watch the children stuff themselves into the trough of the larger tires in the yard and hide there. In the fall, we made heaps of leaves, and then everyone, including Pat and me, flopped down in them and relished the pungent smell. We played "wheel," joining hands in a ring and circling first one way, then the other. This invariably ended with everyone tumbling on everyone else and it was special fun when teacher was at the bottom of the pile and struggled up last.

A "boat" was soon to be added to the outdoor equipment. Pat's husband is a carpenter and was constructing it with all the trimmings.

Often we took the children on trips around the countryside. We stopped at an airport where the children climbed into a real plane and were shown the controls. At a farm, Elizabeth fed a lamb from a bottle, and in the barn, everyone climbed a ladder into the hayloft. Elizabeth had always been a fine climber. Once we had a beautiful walk in the woods and here all the kids including Elizabeth jumped over a small rivulet. But it was Elizabeth who then lay down beside it and ran the water through her fingers and listened to it gurgle and splash.

At times, she had to push aside twigs and branches in order to move forward and she got the feel of a rough path beneath her feet. She listened eagerly to twittering birds and the hum of insects. She smelled the good earth. "This is the woods, Elizabeth," I told her. "The woods is a place where there are lots and lots of very tall trees and many thick bushes. It is the home of birds and insects. You are hearing them talking to each other now."

Later, when school was over, Elizabeth and I went back there just by ourselves and listened again to the sweet sounds of the woods.

We found that rest time is a very important part of the day and should come just before the children help clear up before going home. They stretched out on mats on the floor and covered themselves with blankets while Pat read a story or played a record. Pat and I need this respite too when the children have settled down to quiet or drowsing.

The big reward for me was watching Elizabeth, comfortable and happy, among all these normal carefree children and in so many ways, performing just as easily.

For instance, a balancing feat:

We lined up strong cardboard blocks along the floor, told the children that this was a "bridge" or maybe a "wall" and asked them to walk along it without falling off. The first time Elizabeth tried it, I took her hand and guided her, letting her first feel just where the edges were. After that, she could do it perfectly. Only one other child could do it the first time. I believe that long experience with the importance of the edges of things was a great help to her.

One day she amazed both Pat and me when she went to the blackboard and on request, drew first a very adequate circle, then a straight line. "Now a curvy line," Pat said, and sure enough Elizabeth then produced a curvy line. She also learned to draw her initial E. on the board when all the others were learning to do theirs.

Another time, when I had been busy with the other children, I looked up and discovered that Elizabeth was nowhere to be seen. "Where are you, Elizabeth?" I called. Then I heard a small voice issuing from the toilet, calling happily, "Here I am, Mama." I went and found her comfortably seated just where she should be, mission accomplished! She had noticed that all the others went there independently when they needed to, and after she had had a few guided tours, decided thereafter to travel alone.

But I have to catch myself. I have mentioned and must remember that for some things there is no complete substitute for vision. Together, Pat and I had to devise ways around these or find other occupations for Elizabeth. So while the charts with pictured objects for word discrimination were in use, I might take Elizabeth off by herself for a story. Sometimes, however, I described the pictures to her and got her to listen while the other children picked out one as having a different sound from the others.

Although Elizabeth had had boats to sail in her wading pool, she had not yet perhaps, grasped the idea as had most of the other children, that these are miniature editions of real ones, big enough for people to cross large bodies of water. So'when that large model finally comes and is set up in the yard, it probably would have no meaning for her beyond something new to climb on. Unlike the others, who had seen pictured boats with their great size relative to humans, for Elizabeth a "book" is just something you bring to a person who then tells a story. From stories and her toy boat, she knows that boats are among the things that float in the water. But how big are they? How big is the water?

Elizabeth also had trouble learning to use scissors. This is hard even for sighted children and some seem to learn faster than others. So it is hard to say how much of her struggle with this had to do with her blindness. I expect she will master this eventually but it will take time.

She was partially handicapped too in some of our reading readiness and number concept teaching. As well as counting objects which we did whenever there was a natural occasion for it, we also had the children affix to a felt board varying numbers of circular cut-outs, then asked them to pick out and place beside the circles, the corresponding number-symbol for which there were also cut-outs. "Place three circles on the felt," we would say. "Now place the number '3' next to them." Most of the children mastered this exercise up to five circles and the correct symbols for them. In this way they learned what "oneness," "twoness," "threeness," really represent instead of merely learning to call the symbol by its name but without an understanding of what it stands for. We suspect that a grasp of these basic number concepts early in life may be crucial for a later understanding of mathematics.

For Elizabeth, we decided to withhold the number-symbols and also practice in the recognition of letters. She probably could have learned to recognize them by feel and to give them their right names. But we feared this might confuse matters when, later on she worked with a Braille expert who would know just how to go about it.

Meanwhile, Elizabeth was certainly acquiring number concepts. She had no trouble selecting, on request, the right number of circles.

I confess to some initial trepidations about how Elizabeth would stand the strain of so many new children her own age in strange surroundings. Would this be too much for her? This was one worry.

The first two days of school, Elizabeth started crying at eleven o'clock sharp. Pat had been playing a march on the piano and Elizabeth wanted to keep right on marching even after Pat said it was time to stop. The second day it was the same, only this time she had bells to ring and didn't want either to stop the marching or give up the bells. So what did I do? I did not try to cajole her or persuade her to conform. I simply took her home at once. She was dead tired and no wonder. This was bound, at first, to be a stressful introduction to a new life. But after those first days Elizabeth never cried again at school nor did I ever have to take her home early.

Elizabeth was not the only child who had crying spells at school those first days; and it seemed to me that it might have

been a good idea if those tired little ones too had been able
to leave a bit early until it all became easier for them.

Worry number two:

Would Elizabeth grab things from other children and insist on having her own way? In spite of my efforts to have her
understand the importance of sharing, I wondered whether
what she had learned would stand up in this new situation.
Well, not perfectly. But perhaps she had no more trouble in
this department than others. It takes a long time.

Another worry nagged me:

How would Elizabeth seem to the other children? How
would they feel about her acting a little differently? Would
some of her ways, the result of her blindness, be misunderstood
and antagonize them?

Early in the summer term, I had my chance to tackle this
last problem. We were having a tea-party seated around a
table and Elizabeth's hands started to move in every direction
upsetting cups and plates. Thereupon, arose a din of voices
yelling, "No, Elizabeth!" and Elizabeth kept angrily crying,
"Just leave her alone." This scene was the climax to my
having noticed before that the children eyed her a bit strangely
when she went up to them and started fingering their hair,
hands, and body. Now was the time to act.

We asked all the children to sit quietly and I took Elizabeth on my lap. I asked the children whether they had noticed
that Elizabeth sometimes acted a little differently from them.
When heads nodded, I said that Elizabeth was "blind" and
that this meant that her eyes could not see like theirs. She had
to use her hands to *feel* instead. When she reached for something and touched it, this was her way of "seeing." Then I told
them to close their eyes tight and when they had done this
said that they were seeing just what Elizabeth saw — nothing.

To make it even clearer, we blindfolded all the children,
placed different objects on a table and asked them to tell us
what they were just by feeling. They greatly enjoyed this
game of "seeing with our hands" and it has become a favorite.

Hearing my explanation to the assembled children, Elizabeth, too, perhaps got her first lesson in comprehension of her blindness. Yet, I know that so far, "blind" is only a word to her. It is something she is and others are not. Occasionally, she will go to a child and say, "Are you blind?" Or she puts her hands on my eyes and asks if I can see. I say, "Yes," and leave it at that. It will take a long time for her to understand. For who can comprehend what the world would be like with the addition of a sense one has never possessed?

After this, there was no trouble about Elizabeth being accepted. It was often touching to see how many of the children adjusted to her and tried to help her. For her part, she soon felt a full member of the group, lost her early unwillingness to talk and before long was chattering away with the rest. I noticed that if a child had been absent and had missed some event, it was likely to be Elizabeth who was asked to catch him up and supply the details.

What of the other parents? What did they think of a blind child as a member of this group? Here the children, often so unabashedly direct, helped us out. When their parents came, they sometimes ran up to them and said, "Look, Mom, this is Elizabeth. She is blind. Why can't she see?"

Discomfort and embarrassment on the mother's part! She didn't know how to answer or even how I might feel about it. But also, I fear, there is an unfortunate trait in human character that makes us uneasy and even hostile to whatever is "different," whether it's race, color, language, hair styles or physical peculiarities which we call "abnormal."

I tried to put them at ease. "Yes," I would say, "Elizabeth is blind and has been so from birth. But she has learned to use her other senses and gets along quite comfortably. She is learning here, as all must, to get along in a group of kids her age. It's a great experience for her."

This is apt to break the ice and thereafter the parents can relax and show their interest quite naturally. They begin to see her as she is, a normal little girl who happens to be blind.

Pat tells me that only one mother out of the twelve has

registered a real objection to Elizabeth's being there. Perhaps this is the best score we can expect.

This has been Elizabeth's great year and the new experiences have speeded her development. The main credit, of course, goes to Pat. Though she had had much experience before this as a teacher in the early grades, this was her first year as a nursery school teacher. Naturally resourceful with children, she can always find ways to get them out of a jam and restore good humor and a return to activity. She also senses when not to gloss over the surface of whatever distress a child may be in. She takes time to listen to what may be on his mind that is causing the trouble. She can empathize, actually *feel*, that is, what a child is feeling. This is a priceless gift.

I take a little credit for myself, too, for I had work to do on myself at Sunny Corners.

Before I could do my job right, I had really to understand Pat's very natural misgivings about having Elizabeth in the group. Even when assured of my help, we still had to learn to work together and I had to show that I could be useful to her and to the other children, not just Elizabeth. I had no wish to compete with her special skills as a teacher who must meet the needs of a variety of children, many of them out of their houses for the first time. Then she could accept my superior knowledge of a blind child and we could work together without friction.

At home, a great thing happened in my life, too, that made everything easier. My dear friend Rose, who was with me when Elizabeth was born, offered to come back and help me out with the work in the house. This caused joy all around as well as releasing me both to assist Pat and to find time to write this story.

IV

Now: a Normal Five-Year-Old, Who Is Blind

Elizabeth is now nearing five and the school term is over. In this past year, her development has taken a giant leap. What she does and thinks about now, is much like any child her age. This is the very point I want to make. Though blind, she is also happy and active among her many friends. For the present, she takes her limitations and capabilities for granted. Just as she carried over to nursery school much that she had learned at home, so also she has brought back from Sunny Corners games, skills, and attitudes learned there.

I have had special delight watching Elizabeth's imagination develop. "Pretending" has long been one of her games and I have mentioned some early examples of this.

For instance, after making pancakes at school, this at once became a "pretend" operation at home. That evening when the family was assembled, she announced that we were all to have pancakes. Her preparation of them was accompanied by the appropriate exclamations. "Don't touch the frying pan, it's hot," she said. And then, "Now I have to turn the pancake over." This she did with a pretend spoon.

During music time at school, we used to pretend we were trees. We all raised our arms for branches and swayed to and fro as the wind blew through them. The children planted their feet firmly apart and, as the music showed the wind blowing harder, we all swayed faster. Now Elizabeth wants this game at home, enlisting her brothers and sisters as other trees, while I put a record on.

"Popcorn" was another favorite game at school. We all

crouched on the floor and when Pat played popcorn music, we all became hot and started popping up all over the room. Elizabeth's brothers and sisters find this a little juvenile for their tastes, "silly," they say, and she has a harder time getting them to join her in this one.

Then there was "toboggan." We held to the sides of rubber mats and went swaying around corners and when we hit a bump, everyone fell off. Also "bicycle." The child lies on his back and according to the tempo of the music, his upraised legs pump faster. Now we play this at home.

So many things to learn about your body and all it can do! This is good for any child but especially for one who is blind. You can bend arms from the elbows and from the shoulders — hands from the wrists. Your body can bend forward from the waist until you can touch toes with your fingers. There's no end to body skills and mastery of them brings joy and self-confidence.

Some games are Elizabeth's own inventions. For instance, she takes a block of wood, runs it over her Daddy's face and goes "bzzz" in imitation of his shaving.

Elizabeth also gets a "meal."

One evening she approached me and said, "Do you want breakfast, Mama?" "Sure thing," I answered. "Eggs?" she asked, and when I said yes, she wanted to know whether scrambled or fried. I said scrambled and she said positively, "No, fried." "Okay," I agreed. She then tripped happily to a table, picked out a pan and spoon and brought her own basket of sea shells. One by one she brought these to the table near me and began systematically to hit each shell against the edge of the pan. Then she dumped the lot into the pan and pushed them around with the spoon. After enough "eggs" had been thus "fried," she gave them to me to eat. And how I "ate"! smacking my lips with pleasure.

Oh, how that child delights me! My very greatest delight is watching while she hatches a thought in her mind that's all her own and then sets forth to carry it out.

When Elizabeth was around four and a half, a friend

named "Zene" appeared in her life, strictly her own invention. He has been her imaginery companion ever since and she babbles away about him. Why the name "Zene" is anyone's guess but he is a busy fellow. He is never actually with Elizabeth but goes about his own business elsewhere. He baby-sits, he goes down town or to the movies or he is "upstairs fooling around." He plays cards and takes showers. Sometimes Elizabeth says, "I must go now and find Zene." At times he seems to be more real to her than a tangible doll.

Nevertheless, Elizabeth has become fond of her doll Baby Drowsy. It's fun to pull Drowsy's string and make her talk or cry. Drowsy goes with us to the store or beauty parlor and recently, when I had an appointment with the dentist, we all three went.

Elizabeth had been there when her sisters had appointments but had never had her own teeth checked. This visit was a preparation for things to come. She was offered a ride in the dentist chair which indeed she had already located and had started to climb into. She quickly said yes, and up and down she went. It was great fun, and in her own words, "just like a fair." (The summer before, we had taken her to the county fair and she had a great time riding in the ferris wheel, the merry-go-round, a real pony, and she enjoyed her first taste of cotton candy. The sounds there made a great impression on her and all in all, the fair was a topic of conversation for weeks.)

Soon now, it was I who was in the dentist chair but not alone. Elizabeth remained on top of me and Drowsy on top of her. I wasn't sure how this would work out but my nice young dentist told Elizabeth to stay right there and proceeded to clean my teeth while Elizabeth, lying on my stomach, kept asking, "What's that noise?" and the dentist explained. "Now what are you doing?" she demanded when she sensed that something different was going on; and each time the dentist explained. Then she pulled Drowsy's string and said, "Drowsy wants another drink of water," and the nurse came forward and gave her one. "Shall I look at your teeth too, Elizabeth?"

asked the dentist when he finished with me. "Yes, do," she replied, and as he reached into her mouth she said teasingly, "I'll bite your finger."

After the dentist had examined her teeth, he put a bit of polish on her finger nail and gently ran the polishing brush over it. This tickled and she laughed. Then he gave her a new tooth brush and she was a happy little girl. On reaching home, she grabbed another of her dolls and gave his teeth a going-over. So now when her turn comes for her first real check-up, I think she will welcome the dentist with pleasure instead of fear.

It is impossible to describe everything this busy little girl is up to nowadays, and even harder to say just when certain skills were achieved. Mostly, her earlier activities have matured and become increasingly elaborate.

She makes "pies," holes and hills in the sand box, builds higher and steadier block towers as well as houses and other buildings with doors and windows. She paints, pastes and strings beads with increasing skill, she uses crayons and likes to feel the marks she has made with them on the paper.

She is advancing rapidly in the ability to be a real house-hold helper instead of the pretend one of earlier times. Now she can reliably regulate the hot and cold water and pour water from one container to another. She goes to the laundry room, fetches the mop and pail and proceeds to fill the pail (cup by cup, to be sure). This may result in some spilling but she understands that when this happens, she must wipe it up. She grabs a towel and, with her little hands, feels around for the wet places making sure she has not missed any. She is also learning what every kitchen helper should know — just where the dishes belong and she can put away pots and pans in more or less the right places. If needed, she hauls out the bench that Grandpa made her and knows about where to place it to climb up and replace dishes. She also uses it to reach the cookie jar or canisters into which she dips her fingers to identify flour, sugar or rice. Alas! She can now open the refrigerator door and go exploring. Sometimes this makes

Mama frown, and she hears the frown in my voice. Same with the dishwasher. This is just too much fun for her and I have to put my foot down about this.

Elizabeth is gradually learning to dress herself and can now get into panties, slacks, socks and shirt with very little help. Once, she actually got her coat on right; usually it goes on backward or upside down. This breakthrough was the result of months of plugging away. She washes her face very well and makes an attempt at brushing her hair. Miracle! She is now a decently neat eater and rarely spills.

It is interesting to watch her constantly comparing things. "This is like a ball," she says of anything round. With clay, she makes "spaghetti," "beans," worms," naming them each time.

Her vocabulary and use of words is going ahead fast. While she is playing, it is talk, talk, talk. Slipping up on the use of a pronoun usually comes when she is under stress, like the time when children yelled at her in school for upsetting glasses and plates. Now, she corrects herself, and if she says *"She* wants a drink of water," she hastily adds, "No, *I* want a drink of water."

She is constantly exploring. Only a year ago there was no trouble about her staying in the back yard when she played outdoors. Now she goes out the rear door, zips around to the front of the house, inspects the garage, collects a few stones from the driveway and comes in again through either the front door or the garage. She greatly enjoys this freedom. I do not go out with her but check on her often. She checks on me too to make sure I am still in the house, every once in a while opening a door and hollering, "Mama?" and on hearing my voice, returns again to her play.

We are delighted that Elizabeth wants to stay over night with her grandma. Her first try at this was when my husband and I went out of town and arranged for her to stay with this much-loved person. We telephoned the first night and Elizabeth was all talk. She described everything she had been doing, told us what she had had for dinner, where she was going to sleep. We learned she had been in her nightie hours before bed-time in anticipation of the fun of sleeping in Grandma's bed. Now she keeps asking us when she can repeat this great treat.

A neighbor has a swimming pool and gives regular swimming lessons to children. Last summer, when Elizabeth was four, she took her into the water and gave her a ride on her tummy to give her the feel of the water. She also got her to put her face down in water cupped in her hands and asked Elizabeth to blow into it, thus accustoming her to the sensation of water on her face. Elizabeth is fond of this neighbor and now that she is turning five, will have regular swimming lessons. So far, she shows no fear and it would not surprise me if she learned to swim this coming summer.

More and more, Elizabeth is enjoying her friends and developing definite preferences. At school, she had her special buddies and others she more or less ignored. In the neighborhood, all the store people know her, greet her when we come and the lady at the drive-in-bank says, "Hello, Elizabeth" over the microphone.

But her brothers and sisters are still her greatest pals. The girls especially love fussing with her and helping with clothes and hair. When Terri goes off to college next year, Elizabeth will miss her. Terri is the one who sometimes takes her on her own errands; or they go to Terri's girl friends' houses, where Elizabeth's fluent talk and curiosity about everything around her is a great source of interest to all.

For nearly a year now, beginning when she was just past her fourth birthday, she has been sleeping in a regular twin size bed, sharing a room with Sherri. The night of the big move, we put thick blankets on the floor beside the bed in case she fell out. I thought she might take it hard when she found we had got rid of her beloved crib and that now there was no turning back. But she did not seem to mind, did not fall out of the big bed at any time. Instead, she was thrilled to be promoted to this new status in which she shared a room with her sister.

I have found with my children that the achievement of greater maturity in one field is often carried over to another.

A few weeks after the move to the larger bed, Elizabeth, in school, learned to go to the big toilet by herself. This in turn carried over at home. Here, she had always used her own potty-chair, but soon after these happenings she started going to the toilet like a grown up. Now she not only finds her way to the bathroom; she turns on the light (whether it is night or day) and gets herself up on the toilet by herself after locking the door. When finished, she unlocks it again. She uses reams of toilet paper. What child doesn't?

This daughter of mine is also developing a sense of humor and loves to tease.

One day, she came to me announcing that she had done a B.M. in her pants. I said, "Oh Elizabeth, you know that's not the place for it." Then I felt her panties and sure enough, they definitely felt as if she had done something. She kept a straight face as I escorted her to the bathroom and then, when I pulled her panties down, she started to laugh. What I found was that B.M. was really balls of playdough! We enjoyed the joke together and I reflected on the many uses of playdough. She also puts it sometimes on the end of a stick and say it's a lollipop.

I have been told that psychologists are interested in how blind people dream. Most of us, it seems, dream visually and this would not be possible for a child like Elizabeth. So I took note when Elizabeth, at about four and a half, first reported what must have been a dream and it was no surprise to me that she dreamed in terms of her other senses.

She awoke in the night crying in real distress. I went to her, took her in my arms and asked what troubled her. All she could say was, "She stuck her foot in it and turned it on." I told her I thought she must have had a dream and then did what all mothers do; took her to the bathroom, gave her a drink of water and soothed her back to sleep. Next morning, the dream had changed to "I bumped my foot." She also said, "I had a dream."

I don't know what the dream "means." Let the psychoanalysts make the most of it! I do know that the dream had troubled her for she had reverted to the misuses of the personal pronoun when she first told me of it in the night and this she does only when under stress.

I want also to mention the eye pressing which used to be frequent. Today, this too comes rarely and only at moments of emotional tension. Mostly her hands are too busy with many tasks to be used this way. When she does press her eyes, a simple reminder that "it doesn't look nice" seems to be enough and doesn't make her cross. On the rare occasions when the urge is very strong, I don't make an issue of it.

Elizabeth has her harder moments too. For some reason, she accepted lots of noise and confusion at school without seeming to be greatly bothered by it. At home, it is a different story and turmoil there is likely to trigger a crying spell. At such times, she cries and cries, can't say what's wrong and the only solution is to hold her close and rock her in the rocking chair. Usually, this occurs over week-ends which, as every mother knows, is a time when everything is difficult. Husband and children are all milling about each wanting to do his own thing. In contrast, on week-days, Elizabeth and I have a rather set routine, including a quiet lunch together. But on Saturdays and Sundays, Elizabeth is likely to want one of her records on when another child wants TV — a hopeless conflict. Sometimes too, she presses a brother or sister to do something with her and gets turned down. Also a sudden loud noise can precipitate panic.

She was on the couch one day, when one of the boys came near and clapped his hands very suddenly close to her ear. Though he had not intended to scare her, she was taken by surprise and burst into loud wails. My son was very distressed and I again had to remind him that since Elizabeth cannot see him approach, it would be a good idea to call to her when he is coming and to let her know too when he is going away.

Another problem is guests. Usually Elizabeth enjoys company but not when they bring a lot of strange noisy children. Recently, a friend of mine appeared bringing her four children and soon confusion and shouting reigned. I tried without success to calm things; then Elizabeth came to my friend and said politely, "You go home now," thus echoing my own unspoken sentiments.

But in addition to noise and confusion in her home, there is something else that I am puzzled about how to handle. Angry voices and signs of quarreling scare the living daylights out of her. I believe my family is relatively peaceful but there is no such thing as a bunch of lively youngsters who don't get into each other's hair now and then, yelling and making extravagant threats. Elizabeth tends to take it all quite literally and seems really frightened even when the anger is not directed at her. I explain to the older children that Elizabeth can't understand all this and try to quiet them. I tell Elizabeth that even people who love each other sometimes get angry. But while there is truth in this, it is not the whole truth. One has only to look around the world today to see how tragically easy it is for people and nations to be set against each other and commit acts of hostile aggression. This quickness to hate seems to run deep in human nature — in fact, it is my idea of what is meant by original sin. Eventually, we have to learn to live with a certain amount of it and while working always to reduce it, know that it is a fact of life. We want especially to keep our own homes as free of it as we can while not getting too distressed when it erupts now and then as it is bound to. Elizabeth too must face this and find ways to cope with it instead of panicking.

Another problem, a very practical one, will be with us for a long time. This is the ever present one of striking the right balance between giving her freedom and keeping her from physical harm. Her slow careful way of going about things is some help but cannot be wholly counted on. There come times when quick action is necessary.

Our front yard is on the street where cars pass. I keep plugging away at the dangers here, telling her that the cars she hears coming could hurt her badly unless she always stays on the grass and never ventures alone into the street. I tell her that if she hears a friend drive into our place, she must also remain on the grass and not go to the driveway to meet the car. I get her to repeat all this. Also, when someone leaves, we stand on the grass together until she hears the car drive away. I believe that if one is realistic about real dangers and at the same time shows how they can be avoided, self-confidence, not timidity can be built.

Recently, I was watching Elizabeth when she heard Mark's voice across the street where he was playing ball. I saw her start to go, then stop dead in her tracks. I was very happy about this and went out and praised her for having managed so well. But I cannot count on it. I am constantly on the alert when she is near the street.

She had a fortunate object lesson. Dickie one day forgot his school lunch box and left it in the driveway. Daddy, leaving for work, didn't see it and backed the car over it. We heard the crunch, then Dickie's cries of distress. We went out and I got Elizabeth to examine the box carefully and feel the squashed potato chips and other items scattered here and there. This experience gave her a pretty good idea of the damage a car can do and she mentioned it several times in the days following.

But at the moment, the outdoors question has taken another turn. I know that children go through unpredictable ups and downs, including often developing fears out of the blue. Just now, Elizabeth has suddenly become afraid of the vacuum cleaner when Mark cleans the car with it. Also, the compressor for the air conditioner which goes on and off as needed is located in the back of the house near where she usually plays. This summer, both these sounds seem to terrify her, and although these noises are not foreign to her, she has refused to go outdoors to play. So I have enrolled her again in the summer session of nursery school, this time without Mama! Elizabeth dearly loves Pat and she will find some of her old friends there too. She is very happy to go.

Nursery school on Tuesdays and Thursdays and swimming lessons Mondays and Wednesdays should keep her happily occupied. We will not force the outdoor routine at home. In time, I expect, her fears will fade.

Sex Education

Elizabeth like most children her age has been much interested in her body and nearly a year ago started asking questions.

One evening, she was sitting on my lap feeling my eyes, my mouth, ears and hands. We were comparing. "Elizabeth has eyes; Mama has eyes." Then she went on to her brother. "Dickie has eyes; Dickie has a bottom." I agreed. Then she said, "Dickie has a vagina."

"No he hasn't Elizabeth," I said, "Dickie has a penis instead because he is a boy. You are a girl."

Her doll Pierre is a baby doll, anatomically correct though I must say his boy fixture is quite a bit played down. But he was all I had to work with and shortly thereafter, we dug him out of the play box and I tried to demonstrate the difference between boy and girl. At about this time, a friend of mine was expecting a baby and I kept begging her please to have a boy as I needed a real live boy baby for Elizabeth to feel. It wasn't long before there came a phone call saying that my friend had had not one boy baby but two! We had struck a gold mine.

So I took Elizabeth to see the twins when they got home from the hospital and when one of them was having a bath Elizabeth was delighted to meet a really tiny baby and when she had felt the little boy body all over was even more interested in the fact that he had to wear diapers, drink from a bottle and cried quite a lot. Then she set off to explore my friend's house.

No big thing was made of this "lesson," but I believe that her personal discovery of this basic difference in the sexes will stay with her and be used as needed.

How about the bodies of grown-ups?

In the late afternoons, I usually take a shower and don't like to lock Elizabeth out. Partly, this is because there is no one else in the house at this time but also, it is because I remember I never locked any of my children out at this age. If I had tried to, they would have knocked the door down with pounding and yelling to come in. I know one draws the line somewhere, but that point seemed to come naturally. Nevertheless, it does seem that mothers give up a good deal of privacy when children are young.

So when I stepped out of the shower I occasionally let Elizabeth feel me and she enjoyed discovering how wet I am. She would feel my legs and my buttocks—and then I have thought, "Well, why not?" and let her feel my breasts. This has led to my telling her that her sister Terri has breasts too and so do Grandma and Betty and someday she will too. But people like her brothers or Daddy do not have them because they are boys or men. This is as far as her explorations and questions have gone.

I have met all my children's questions of this kind in about the same general way, varying with how much interest they show. I am a firm believer in sex education, preferably at home, but if not there, then at school. All our children have asked how babies are made. Learning that they grow in the mother's stomach, they are likely to ask first, how they get out, and quite a bit later, how they get in. We have had such things come up at the breakfast table and have answered them then and there. But we limit our answers to what really seems to be on the child's mind and don't tell a lot more than he wants to know.

Dickie was eight when he asked one morning how babies get into the mother's tummy. I reminded him of what he already knew that boys and girls were made differently and I presented this as God's plan.

"God made men and women different," I told him, "so that when they love each other a great deal, they can have what is called sexual intercourse. The man can put his penis into the woman's vagina and some fluid called semen comes out and flows into her body. There it may meet a tiny egg in her body and because the semen is something like fertilizer, it makes the seed grow into a baby."

Hearing this, Dickie looked at me with a very comical

expression on his face and asked, "Is that what you and Daddy did?" I said "Yes, and so did all the parents you know. So did Grandma and Grandpa and that's how Daddy was made and everyone else."

Dickie considered all this carefully, then exclaimed, "Boy, I never knew that before!" Later, my husband and I had a good chuckle over that one.

This is how we approach such matters in our family and so I expect we will with Elizabeth too when the time comes. I'm not saying it's the only right way. Parents have to discover what is most comfortable for them.

I suspect that the most important factor in children's sex education is not the facts they learn. It is the quality of the relationship between their parents which they are sure to sense. All our children are aware how hard Daddy works to make a family comfortable and they see that I do my part too. They know we love each other. The other day when my husband kissed me, Elizabeth called out, "Daddy kissing Mama." Daddy then went to Elizabeth and gave her the kind of kisses that come a hundred to the second — rapid-fire type. She laughed and wiggled happily. She found it very pleasant to be loved.

When Elizabeth was four years and eight months old, we drove her to Ann Arbor for a developmental check-up which the Project gives at regular intervals to all the children they have been watching from early infancy. Currently, there are seventeen and Elizabeth is the oldest. Psychologists and students in training are present on these occasions, a sound film is made of her behavior in various situations, the voice — articulations and words — are tape recorded and these can then be studied and discussed by the staff and students, thus contributing to their knowledge of how children, blind from birth, can develop.

For us, this was a very happy occasion. Elizabeth was delightful. To all of us, she seemed to have left babyhood behind. Now she was quite a little lady, even to the point of some self-consciousness and playing up to the audience, evidences of a desire to be on her good behavior.

She walked into the room with Drowsy tucked under her arm. With this old friend she could feel secure and she hung onto her until she thawed out. Drowsy proved to be an important part of the record because she was far more important to Elizabeth than the doll in last year's film. Now Elizabeth got Drowsy to play a doll size piano in various ways. She would announce, "Now she will play the piano with her feet" and after that, Drowsy did the same with her head and finally her hands. All this was in response to requests from the psychologist.

We had brought a small blackboard. Elizabeth felt the corners and when questioned, said there were four. Again on request, she did as she had done in school, drew first a circle, then a straight line, then a wiggly line.

To show hand coordination, there was a sequence of her unscrewing the top of her vitamin bottle from which she took out exactly one pill, offered it to the psychologist and then screwed the top on again.

Next, she was given playdough and some dried beans in a saucepan with a spoon. She at once asked for a rolling pin and when this was supplied, rolled out pieces of dough, wrapped the beans in them and said she was making "friends." She also made cookies with these materials.

At last came a large plastic tub filled with water. I had assured her that she would have a chance for some water play which she dearly loves and she had been waiting patiently. What followed was very funny to watch. Talking continuously about what she was doing, she first dumped a doll in (not Drowsy) for a bath, then threw it away forgotten. Then she removed her shoes and socks and very gingerly, dipping one foot in, announced that the water was cold and pretended to shiver. She leaned over the water, said it was "like a pool" and that the water was "cloudy." She rubbed her legs, saying they were "dirty." Then, seeing she would never be satisfied until she could actually get into the tub, I removed her dress and slip. She at once got in and started to sit down but finding the seat of her pants wet, patted them and said, "It's like going to the potty in your panties." This brought much laughter from the observers.

After all this, when dressed again, she sat at a table, ate pretzels, drank milk, gave pretzels to the psychologist. She counted walnuts; she sang softly while "playing the guitar," Later she climbed the monkey bars.

Once I left the room for a minute and watched her through a window. Elizabeth soon asked for me and was told that I had left the room but would be back soon. At intervals, she asked for me a few times more and received the same answer. Then the psychologist asked, "Do you think Mama will be back?" and Elizabeth answered "Yes."

There was no doubt in our minds that Elizabeth was now ready to go to kindergarten. Her preparation for someday entering public school had begun the day we were told she was blind, and for the past three years I have been seizing opportunities to let the people at the local school get acquainted with her. That was one motive for having her visit her sister's classroom when she was just past two. To help us further, one of the Ann Arbor staff came to show before a group of administrators and elementary school teachers a film showing a young blind girl attending a regular public school class for normal children. They were interested, and because they also knew a bit about Elizabeth I thought I had reason to be hopeful.

But, to make a long story short, I met with defeat here. The local school which I was eager to have Elizabeth attend has refused to accept her. The refusal is based on a combination of "regulations" and limited funds. Though the state is obligated under the law to provide appropriate education to handicapped children, this need not necessarily be in their home towns. So when Elizabeth is just past five, she will be bussed twelve miles to the nearest large town where there is a kindergarten and lower grade school for handicapped children. Fortunately it is located in a class-room attached to the regular public school so that the children can go back and forth and learn to know each other. Elizabeth is to be in a morning kindergarten for the visually handicapped. A Braille teacher will begin work with her.

If I had any assurance that later, Elizabeth could go on in the upper grades of our local school, this would not be a bad solution; I can only hope. I dislike bussing for children. Besides the wear and tear, I fear she will miss out on friendships that develop naturally among neighbor kids when they go to school together. Now, as things stand, she must be parted from the friends she made this year at nursery school, all of whom will be going on to our local kindergarten. For the present, I must rest content with the knowledge that the school Elizabeth will attend is a good one and that she will have expert instruction.

Do we ever think of someday sending her away from home to a special school? Certainly not until she is much older and has gained the inner strength that comes from family and small town life. After that, only time can tell what will best meet her needs. We do not rule it out.

This past winter we received a notice of the first Statewide Conference for Parents of Preschool Blind Children. I lived in happy anticipation of this event and the opportunity to meet parents with children like our own. My husband and I drove, over all, a hundred and eighty miles to attend it. Many of the other parents had come long distances too. This was the first conference of its kind and although it was for us somewhat painful, I believe much was learned that can be put to good use in the future.

What was so distressing was to hear again and again that a blind child has to be taught to chew, that many of these children could not walk even when far beyond the age when this can be expected, that many more were not talking and some who had talked, were regressing again to silence.

Another time, I was invited to attend a workshop concerned with the education of the blind. It started by our having our eyes bandaged so that we did not have even light perception, after which we were asked to feel our way around. I found this quite an unnerving experience — but it aroused also, a great new surge of admiration and tenderness for my wonderful little girl.

Most recently, I was asked by an instructor in the Special Education Department at Western Michigan University to give a talk on the development of the blind infant to a group of college students. I accepted, and found the atmosphere informal and comfortable and I believe it was a success. Afterwards, one of the students asked if she might work with Elizabeth on walking the balance beam, some other special exercises and perhaps swimming. Feeling it would be fun, I agreed, and have arranged to take her to the college gym for as long as things seem to go well.

This was an especially gratifying experience. And to think that I nearly refused to go because that first phone call asking me to, came at a moment when I was very tired!

"Cissy"

Recently, we have expanded our family group and took the big step of adding a foster child to our family. Cissy is sixteen years old. Because she was badly neglected by her own parents, she was finally made a ward of the Juvenile Court.

I first knew Cissy as a member of my catechism class where she was loud and aggressive. Yet something about her appealed to me and touched my heartstrings. Later, I heard that the foster home she was then in could not keep her and that she had been returned to the Juvenile Home.

I could not get this child out of my head and talked about her to my husband. He urged me to find out more about her and see if there was some way we could help. I also talked to my children about the possibility of having Cissy come to live with us until Terri said, "Stop talking about it, and do it."

A long conference with the psychiatrist at the Child Guidance Clinic followed. He gave me all the red flags for the plan. Cissy had a sad history; she had certainly been around! The big question was whether she was undamaged enough to be able to accept and trust the love we wanted to give her. The psychiatrist was obviously sizing me up too. Eventually, he decided I might be able to "make it" with her. He believed this child needed loving discipline and teaching, plus the example of my other children in accepting reasonable standards of behavior.

Since she came to us, it hasn't been all a bed of roses. Cissy is loud and bossy, prone to put in her two cents worth if I have to reprimand another child. Once this led me to say, "Look, who's the mother around here anyway?" She is also inclined to a kind of rough slap-stick teasing which my children don't care for at all. The time came when Mark lost his cool and gave her a resounding smack. Another time, Dickie shouted, "Go back to that Juvenile Home!" to which Cissy replied, "I don't want to."

On such occasions, I keep an ear cocked but don't interfere. I suspect Cissy can learn more from my children than from me.

Gold stars for my sons! This kind of talk and "play" has greatly diminished.

But Cissy also has a lovable side. She may sit on the floor by my side and lean against me and then, if I put a hand on her arm or touch her cheek, I see tears in her eyes.

One day, she made Terri's bed for her as a "surprise" and beamed all over when later Terri thanked her.

Very important — Elizabeth likes Cissy and Cissy seems really to love Elizabeth. With this child, Cissy has a chance to "feel superior" for once, and discover that she can really be needed and useful. These are experiences she desperately needs.

Only time will tell how all this will work out. I am to keep in touch with the psychiatrist.

In the Fall, Cissy will go to high school where she will encounter rules and some demand for conformity. I hope and pray — but so far, I am not discouraged.

Me, Myself

How I manage my own life is very important too. I am sure that Elizabeth must not have a mother who is a martyr or a slave. Since I have many friends as well as relatives, it is not hard for me to lead an active, informal social life. One should not always be with children. We adults need our own age-group too.

Some work in the community is a "must," I believe, for the full life, and I have spoken of my increasing concern for blind children everywhere. I also do quite a bit for my church where I have had classes in the catechism. I help at church suppers. I belong to a group of church members who are taking on some of the routine business work of the parish to leave the priests free to give more time to their spiritual role. And many other things come along to which I want to say yes.

Recently, my husband and I had a wonderful trip to Montreal. We engaged a couple we know very well to come and stay with the children while we were away. Terri was quite hurt that we would not leave the whole household to her and I am sure she could have managed. Her time will come, but we thought it was not quite yet.

There is also one's own interior life. Since Elizabeth's birth I have gone occasionally, for a few days, to a Retreat located on a beautiful lake. Here, free for a time of mundane things, I refurbish my soul, mind, and body. Last time, we listened to some wonderful talks that gave much food for thought; we had lazy walks in the pine woods. We talked together, prayed and thanked God for giving us faith and for making us happy people. In peace and quiet you can think things out. It's a good way to rid yourself of any hangups you may have.

I give much thought to what ideals I have for my children.

My dearest hope is that we can rear them so they will have love in their hearts for their fellow man and that they will feel impelled to translate this into action. In turn, they will pass these values on to their children and so down the generations. I want each one to feel that he is truly worth something and so has something to give. But for myself, it is also true that I have a special feeling for blind babies and their parents wherever they are and pray that the day will come when, for each one, there will be someone waiting to say, "We want to help you," instead of their being left to stumble alone in the darkness.

V

Postscript

As I close this story, I find myself troubled for fear I have not adequately put my message across.

Have I made it all sound too easy? It has not been.

In telling of my real joy in Elizabeth have I also had times when I was bone-tired, or cross, or neglectful of others? Yes, I have. If I seem inconsistent, I can only say that both the joy and the discouragement have been real.

In darker moments, both my husband and I have feared for what is ahead though we rarely mention this to each other. What will it be like for Elizabeth when, in spite of all, she discovers that she is "different"? Will she ever marry and have children of her own? If not, will she be able to make for herself a life that is nevertheless fulfilled? We can only hope and try to help each small step of the way.

I have stressed the value of rearing a blind child on many of the same principles as a normal sighted child and have given bits of my own philosophy about this. But there are real differences, too. Development in the blind is slower, often discouraging, and nothing can be left to chance. Vision itself is the great teacher of the sighted child. Hearing and the other senses never make up for this deficit unless one marshals them fully and works with them constantly, beginning in the first weeks of life.

I am also convinced that the very early rapport between mother and child lays the groundwork for everything that follows, that though it may be harder to achieve with a blind baby, one must not give up. When achieved, it may result in a longer period of mother-dependence but this should be welcomed as a sign of emotional health. When the time comes, the child can be helped to work out of it.

I have been fortunate in many ways — fortunate that when Elizabeth came I had already had experience with four children. I hope that much that I have learned may be of help to others. The task is always how best to guide a child to the fulfillment of *his* capabilities whether these be great or small.

Some people are scornful or cynical about "the experts." We are not. They are among our precious resources. Here, too, we have been fortunate, for our experts have been warm human beings, infinitely helpful.

What do we plan to tell Elizabeth when the time comes to explain her blindness to her? We will *not* tell her that God willed it; or that the doctors did it. When she is old enough to understand that she is a living miracle and that her own kind of life, "different" in certain ways from others, has wonderful rewards. We will, I think, say that the oxygen she was given at birth, enabled her to live but also caused her blindness.

This today is what we plan to say. But we cannot look too far ahead.

Our motto must always be: one day at a time.

Commentary

"Just treat him like any other child and he'll turn out all right."

It is hard to know exactly what is meant by this not very useful but often quoted advice. If it means a blind child has the same human needs as any child, that is obviously true. But if it leads parents to expect their blind child to develop at the same rate and in all the same ways as sighted children, the result is most likely to be misunderstanding and discouragement. The families we met were ready to summon all their resources of affection and understanding on behalf of their blind infants, even in the midst of grief and despair. Nevertheless, without some way of knowing that they were doing the right thing, that the baby was making good progress, hope and effort would be hard to sustain. Raising a blind baby can be a lonely experience. One of the difficulties lies in not having the familiar guidelines from past experience or from the children of people we know.

Perhaps the greatest help to parents at such a time is the knowledge that they *can* learn to understand their blind baby, that all the problems that arise don't have to be solved at once. Learning about development can keep pace with the baby's growth and it isn't necessary to be right every single moment. As our own research at the Child Development Project progressed, we were gathering information from each of the families whose babies we visited. Each family contributed to and shared the new findings about the unique adaptive problems of the blind infant. We described and explained our understanding of the similarities and differences between the early develop-

94

ment of blind and sighted infants. We assured them that the blind baby who is otherwise normal, will use his good intelligence fully, and by school age will be able to do many of the things a sighted child does. But the blind child would need their affection and special guidance to do so. We found the fathers of the blind babies to be very much concerned and involved. In spite of their own work schedules they often found a way to be at home during our visits, even briefly, "just to be there." They too were eager to know how the baby was doing. They had their own questions to ask. They wanted to tell us themselves of some of the baby's latest accomplishments. With increased knowledge about infant development and the special needs of the blind baby, fathers and mothers together could share a justifiable pride in their baby's progress and in the fact that they had been able to be good parents under unusual circumstances.

Human Attachment

"How will he know me?" is one of the first questions parents of blind children may ask us. Reading Elizabeth's story, we see how voice and touch and physical closeness can create the same kind of exclusive love and joy between a blind baby and his parents as that of a sighted baby for his human partners. But this does not happen without special effort. The parents of a blind baby face the task of helping their baby associate mother's and father's voices and bodies with the recurring pleasures of being fed, bathed, or played with. The ordinary events of each day bring many opportunities for holding a little baby and talking to him. Soon the baby begins to connect his parents' voices with the comfort and cuddling he has enjoyed in their arms. Some time after three months he can show us unmistakably that he "knows" his parents. It is quite simple to demonstrate. When we, the interested visitors, speak to him or call his name he quiets down and listens soberly. There is no smile, no vocal response. But if mother or father speak to the baby they are rewarded at once with a beautiful smile and lovely baby sounds obviously meant just for them. No one could question that the ties between parent and baby are being formed and at the same age as for sighted children.

When we consider the large part played by vision in the establishment of human bonds during infancy, we can appreciate the extraordinary problem a blind baby and his parents must overcome. Eye-to-eye contact is the basis of the usual signal system that evolves between mother and child. The baby's smile in response to the human face, the selective smile for the face of mother, father and siblings, the entire sequence of experiences leading to love and recognition of human partners is organized largely through vision in the case of the sighted child.

Through our studies of blind babies we have learned that voice and touch also serve to bring a baby and his parents together. We have been able to use this knowledge to help parents find a tactile-auditory "language" to share with their blind baby and thus to ensure that he will truly "know" them. Knowing his parents, responding to them and returning their love, is the most important and essential event in a young baby's life. Until a baby has found interest and meaning in the world through his beloved human partners no educational strategies can succeed. No toy will have value if the people around him are not valued. For the blind baby, no device can give meaning to sound if the human voice has not united sound with the entire experience of tactile intimacy, comfort and pleasure that can only be provided by an affectionate human partner. It is clear then that the promotion of close ties between the blind baby and his parents must always be our first concern and our most prized accomplishment.

Like all babies, a blind baby has a hunger for experience. As parents learned how to make themselves available to their blind infant through voice and touch, the baby responded with smiles and cooings and wrigglings that we all know to be the first demonstrations of love. Once this "dialogue" of signals and response between parent and blind baby has been created we know we have achieved the first guarantee for the blind baby's development.

Each family had to find its own way. Elizabeth found herself in a house that was filled with voices. If her parents or her four brothers and sisters were not talking to her, they were talking near her, and frequently about her and what she was doing. Mrs. Ulrich enjoys talking to babies. She usually kept up a running commentary to Elizabeth whenever she was with her. She also had a song for almost every occasion. Baby Elizabeth had a large and appreciative audience when she contributed her own "remarks" to the conversation. As Mrs. Ulrich has described it so well, from these beginnings came the steps to real conversation.

For some parents, however, our suggestions about talking to a baby who was only one or two months old made no sense or was not easy to follow. Not everyone finds it natural to "talk" to tiny babies. What do you talk about anyway? Some things are better done than described. Instead of repeating the advice, we offered simple demonstrations during our visits. Since there wasn't a baby we weren't eager to spend time with, nothing could have stopped us from telling a baby how lovely he looked, how becoming his new outfit was, and how we could tell how much he had grown since last time. We took the liberty of speaking for him, putting into words what we thought he was feeling when he looked particularly delighted or uncertain or angry. We discussed the relative merits of one rattle over another and how clever he was to hold it in just that way or to refuse a substitute for the one he really preferred. Then there were the ever ready topics of the weather, the miserable conditions of the highways, or what to have for supper. As the babies responded, according to their age and temperament, as they became quiet to listen and then became more active and vocal, parents came to understand and appreciate the vital importance of linking experience with words, of making their presence known through voice.

A sighted baby who is not often spoken to may be quiet and a little slow to use words, but he does not lose his parents every time they are silent, and he can know of their affection from the many smiles he sees directed toward him. Mother and sighted baby can exchange glances dozens of times a day without saying a word, and feel that they are in touch with each other. The blind child needs to feel in touch with his parents dozens of times a day as well. His parents' voices become very important to him. Once a family realized how much their little baby listened for their voices, they also noticed with some surprise how well he was able to read their moods and know when they were angry or pleased. When Daddy came home from work and called "Hello" from the doorway, he was greeted with much excitement and the demand to be picked up for the rough-housing play that fathers do best. When something was not quite right, when a toy just wouldn't do what he wanted it to, or when he bumped himself slightly in moving around, mother's voice from across the room would often be enough to comfort him and let play continue. We would get many reports that the babies were showing recognition of other sounds. Always these were the sounds that were most important to a baby, footsteps approaching the crib which meant that mother was coming to pick him up, toys being strung above him for play which meant that something interesting was going to happen, the top being screwed on his bottle which meant a comfortable feeding in his mother's arms. We all became more attentive to the sounds around us when we began to listen from the baby's point of view.

At our first meeting with a family, we encourage the parents to hold their blind babies, to offer their physical presence frequently through the day. Not everyone enjoys holding babies and not all babies enjoy being held at first. With time and patience, however, ways can be found to overcome beginning difficulties. Mrs. Ulrich has described how she had to work tenderly and persistently to help Elizabeth adjust to being held in her mother's arms and actually to enjoy being there. It was as important for Mrs. Ulrich to feel her tiny daughter snuggle comfortably against her as it was for Elizabeth to know the comforting presence of her mother. Another less experienced mother took her baby's initial stiffening as a sign that he did not want to be held and therefore should not be held. She did not pick him up and she fed him with a propped bottle. Naturally, she felt shut out and rejected by the baby. We were concerned. Mother and baby were in danger of remaining strangers to each other. An important element in the signal system between this baby and his parents was in jeopardy. He would lose this earliest and most natural way of "knowing" his mother and in associating pleasures and satisfactions with her person. During a morning visit to the home we watched the baby being bathed, dressed and fed. He was, of course, held many times during this flow of activity. There were any number of times when he did seem comfortable in his mother's arms for a short period. As these opportunities came along we commented on the signs the baby gave us that showed he was happy to be held and we encouraged the mother to keep on trying, to build on these small moments. It took time but in a few weeks it was obvious how much more relaxed he was on his mother's lap compared to his polite but somewhat stiff tolerance of us if we picked him up. He not only enjoyed his mother's lap now, he could tell the difference between one lap and another. Having learned the cues to look for, mother and father would then begin noting that the baby responded very differently when he was held by different friends or relatives. He was completely at ease with the lady next door and reached up to feel her face and hair. One fond cousin couldn't hold him even for a minute. For some reason, the baby didn't like that cousin and would protest and cry vigorously. In Grandpa's lap, he began jiggling up and down, trying to get a familiar bouncing game going. Through these social and interpersonal exchanges, the baby became more and more a member of his family.

Being held and carried about provided other essential stimulation as well, stimulation which would have to make up for lack of vision. The sighted baby also needs his fair share of holding. But when he is left lying alone or sitting up by himself he can find much that is of interest just by looking around. He can see his mother at a distance and all the many things that lie beyond reach but are within sight. Vision can organize the separated segments of his experience and constantly calls his attention to the external world. The blind baby's first experiences of the external world have to come from direct contact and begin at the center of his world in his parent's arms. The wealth of stimulation the baby receives when he is held on a lap, shifted to lean against a shoulder, carried about or bumped up and down for a "pony ride" cannot be provided in any other way. As we change our position or his, he has to respond with his entire body. As he is held for play or for his bottle he has the chance to feel the different textures of skin and clothing, of himself and another person. His fingers explore and find buttons, a belt buckle, a watch band. A tremendous amount of learning is taking place while he is "just being held." It is basic learning that must occur first with the people who mean most to him.

Much of this kind of learning can take place at feedings. Baby and mother are together and work in harmony to empty countless bottles of milk and numberless jars of baby food. They adjust to each other to find the way that is best at that particular meal. Holding a baby for his bottle is most important in the early months. Letting him learn to feed himself becomes the important task toward the end of the first year. But the mother of a blind baby may find this period more difficult than the mother of a sighted baby. This is yet another instance where the signal system between the blind baby and his mother may go awry. No mother of a sighted baby needs to "decide" when to introduce self-feeding. A sighted baby has been grabbing everything for months. He is excited and active at mealtime and reaches out for the spoon, the jar of baby food or the bowl of cereal. When teeth appear he chews on his fingers and on toys and on crackers, on whatever feels good. He does not wait for his mother's decision that he is ready. In his own messy and clumsy way he gradually moves toward independence at the table.

The blind baby is just as capable as the sighted baby

of beginning to feed himself toward the end of the first year. But he is less likely to know about all that lies just beyond his reach. He may not give his mother the signal for "Let me feed myself." If the spoon and bowl and cup are always kept at a safe distance, if he is told to keep his hands out of the way, the blind baby will learn to wait passively for each spoonful to be fed. He will have no idea of where the food is coming from and will have no way of understanding or recognizing the complex of activities that lead up to spoon-with-food at his lips. If he is not permitted to bring toys to his mouth when he is playing or when he is teething and wants something to chew on, another chance to pave the way for self-feeding will have been lost.

Blind babies who have missed the chance to learn self-feeding at the most natural and easiest time become very difficult to teach at an older age. Refusal to chew and inability to self-feed at two and three years is often reported in the literature on blind children. We did not find these problems with the children we saw. Some were slower than others to accept solids. Learning to use fork and spoon did take longer. But by the time they were one, almost all the children we saw enjoyed feeding themselves the kinds of foods that are easily picked up by hand and were interested in sampling whatever the family had for dinner.

When a baby could sit up to be fed, at about six months, we suggested that some finger foods be placed within reach during meals, that he be given his own spoon to hold and bang and put in his mouth, that his hand be allowed to follow the course of the spoon that mother held, to track the path from bowl to mouth and back to bowl. Simple advice, but not to everyone's taste. For some mothers this meant slower and messier mealtimes in an already busy day. Or, when the immediate family did not mind the baby's wholehearted participation in a feeding, friends or relatives might be distressed and openly critical of the way he was "playing with his food." But mannerly, well-coordinated table skills simply do not happen without a long period of learning. Mr. Ulrich once commented

that all learning has to go step by step and feeding is no different. He thought sighted children could be pretty sloppy about
it too at first, but people either don't notice or are less upset by
that. They seem to demand more of the blind infant, which is
hardly fair. We know that if we give the blind child a good
chance to learn self-feeding as early as possible, when the time
comes to celebrate his first or second birthday, he will help
himself to his full portion of chocolate cake with icing and
cookies and a glass of milk or pop.

At the end of the first year each baby had demonstrated
the kind of exclusive attachment to his parents that parallels
that of the sighted child. This was a major achievement without
vision to help. Differential smiling and vocalization in the
blind child followed the sequence for sighted children. Discrimination between mother and stranger was clearly demonstrated in the second half of the first year. Reactions of grief
were seen in relation to brief separations from the mother.
Naming "Mama" and "Dada" began early in the second year,
following closely the developmental norms of sighted children.
During his second year he would strengthen and test these
bonds. From this secure relationship within the family he would
later advance to new relationships outside the family as fond
friend and apt student.

Play with Toys

"The baby just doesn't seem to be interested in playing with
any toys."

Until they can get about by themselves little babies depend
pretty much on what adults provide for them in the way of play
things. The possibilities that are likely to present themselves
to the blind infant are considerably fewer than they are for
the sighted babies. The blind infant will spend much of the
first year of his life with no real substitute for the exciting and
continuous visual panorama we take for granted. Things that
he does directly encounter with fingers or mouth have a way
of appearing suddenly or disappearing completely. Until he

becomes mobile, which will be later for the blind child than for the sighted, he has very few ways of finding out about all that exists beyond arm's length. In the sighted child patterns of reaching and grasping develop gradually over the first four to six months when eye and hand become progressively coordinated. We had once assumed that the coordination of ear and hand would help the blind baby reach out to grasp at the same age. To our surprise this was not so. We discovered that for even the most clever and alert totally blind baby, there is no adaptive substitution of sound for sight in intentional reaching, until the last quarter of the first year.

Eye-hand coordination in the sighted child provides a nucleus of behaviors from which many patterns of infant learning evolve. If the corresponding nucleus of ear-hand coordination does not occur until four or five months later for the blind child, we can readily see that this must have important effects on his early and subsequent development. Moreover, just as the sighted baby will be slow to achieve eye-hand coordination without sufficient early stimulation, so will the blind infant be delayed in achieving ear-hand coordination without previous adequacy of stimulation. Compared to the world of the sighted infant, the blind infant's world is relatively impoverished and remains so for a longer time. If we do not find ways to bring interesting outside stimulation to him, many hours of his day will be dull and uninteresting. It is difficult to become interested in things when they exist only during undependable chance contact. For most of the first year, what he is not directly in touch with does not exist. Sounds are still disembodied and do not yet mean to him that there is something "out there" to play with. When something he is holding drops or rolls away, it vanishes completely and he is left with nothing to do, with nothing of interest outside of himself.

The group of blind babies we followed from birth did enjoy playing with toys and were showing definite preferences for favorite toys by the middle of the first year. We took time to discuss with the parents the importance of play experiences even in the earliest months, before most people expect *any* baby to know or care about things. We asked them to think of ways to create an interesting space close to the baby, in front of his chest, within arm's reach; a place where the random movements of an active infant would bring him in touch with a toy that was easy to hold and that made an interesting sound. We stressed the importance of ensuring that the blind baby does find pleasure in toys and other inanimate objects. Learning about the ways in which the things were different from each other and separate from himself and his actions upon them would lead him to the organization of "self-other" experience and knowledge.

Sometimes doubtful, but willing to try anything for the baby's sake, parents would tentatively put our suggestions into effect. In the crib or at the play table or in the playpen, a wonderful assortment of toys and other objects began to appear, always placed so that they remained within easy reach and could not "disappear." Before the baby was ready to sit up he could enjoy toys hanging above him over his chest. A cradle gym or any likely toy that would be easy for small hands to grasp would do. If it did not rattle or tinkle or jangle by itself, we added a few small bells. When the baby was awake his play things could be hung over him for short play times and his waving arms would then bring him new sensations of touch and sound. If there were different shapes hanging side by side, after a while we could see that he was learning to use a different grasp for the thin ring than for the round ball. He seemed to be listening to hear the sounds made by the toys when he shook them or stopped shaking them. When he let go these objects did not fall out of reach but were easily found time and again. This simple play was really quite complex. It encouraged practice in reaching for and grasping objects, in manipulating them in many different ways. It gave the baby essential experience in organizing the area at the midline with both his hands. He could also enjoy rattles or squeaky toys placed in his hands when he was being held for a while after his bottle or bath. A toy too large to grasp could be held in front of him by mother or father to be explored with his finger tips, again creating a situation where the toy would not suddenly vanish but would stay put as long as he was interested in it.

When the baby was able to sit with support, playing at a table surface was a help in providing a new kind of "interesting space." It was important that there be some way to keep toys from falling out of reach. A play table with a rail around the outside edge would keep things in place and the baby could make new discoveries about the toys that were now on a firm flat surface before him instead of hanging loosely in mid-air as they were in the crib. The blind baby who has had several months of play experiences with a cradle gym will sweep his arms towards each other across the table top, certain that something is to be found in the space in front of him. He will go on to find new ways of playing, of manipulating and exploiting the possibilities of play in the new situation. A playpen can be used any time during the first year as a play area where toys can be hung as they are in the crib. Toward the end of the first year the entire inside of a playpen can become a world for the baby to explore, another larger "interesting space" where once again he learns that he can find things and play freely with them, that they will remain somewhere within reach. Toys attached to the top of each side of the playpen make for interesting discoveries when he is old enough to pull himself to a stand and walk around while holding the rail. Before much longer the playpen will no longer contain him and he will be ready to explore the larger territory of the house, confident that this new space will be just as interesting as the spaces that he already has explored.

Some of the children learned a great deal by feeling things with their mouths. Some did not. There is as much variety among blind children as among sighted children. We learned to respect these individual differences and encouraged each family to let their child play with things in a way that seemed to give him the most pleasure and information. By the end of the first year, we could see the development of preference, recognition and memory. Karen was offered a wooden hoop, a solid cube and a musical rattle. She held and shook each in turn, dropped the hoop and cube, and kept the rattle to play with. It was more interesting because it made a sound. Richie recognized his favorite squeaky soldier after a long absence; on one visit it had been gathered up with our play materials by mistake. Two weeks later we returned it, with apologies. Richie happily snuggled the soldier against his chest with both hands. We tried in vain to interest him in a similar toy from our collection. He wanted his own. If a favorite toy was in a basket with several others, Jackie would pull out the others one by one until he found what he was searching for. By the end of the first year play with toys was bringing the children the experiences they needed to begin learning about the objective qualities of inanimate objects, and that objects continue to exist even when they are not heard or felt. Robbie explored the details of a dinner bell, feeling the wooden handle, the cold metal bowl, finding the clapper inside the bowl. He shook it and listened to the sound, then felt it carefully again. He was lucky enough to have a transistor radio to play with. At fifteen months he could switch it on and off intentionally, making the music start and stop.

Toys not only provide varied sense experiences in the impoverished world of the blind child but playing with toys teaches causality and effectiveness which are essential for the blind child in constructing an objective world. The sense of "me" and "other" which emerges first in relation to human objects will be strongly reinforced through an experience with toys and inanimate objects. The blind child, under the most favorable circumstances, is slow to develop a sense of voluntariness, of intentionality, of being a "causer" of events. After his parents and other beloved persons, his toys can help him make vital discoveries about himself, his body and the independent laws that govern the quality of inanimate objects.

When a blind baby's waking hours are filled with interesting activity his sleeping schedule will be similar to that of a sighted baby at the same age. The children in our sample did not sleep an unusual amount. In the second year they were beginning to drop one nap and there began to be the usual problems about going to sleep at night. They did not want to give up all the interesting activities even when they were tired and ready for bed. A bed toy, something to cuddle or play with quietly while dropping off to sleep, could be a comfort when the rest of the world was shut away.

Locomotion

"Will the baby learn to walk?"

Creeping and walking are signs to everyone that a baby is growing up, ready to be more on his own. Somehow as soon as a baby takes his first steps he looks older and wiser. The blind babies we observed from birth seemed, so far as posture and balance were involved, to be ready to creep and to walk at the same age as sighted babies. But for most of them there was a delay of up to five months in creeping, a delay of up to seven months in taking first steps.

The delay in walking, when it occurred, was easier to understand. Even the sighted baby who can see both the floor where his feet will be placed, and his mother waiting to catch him in her open arms just a few steps away, wears a breathless expression of terror and triumph when he first launches forth. The blind child who knows the floor through touch needs much more courage and confidence to keep contact with only the bottom of one tiny foot at a time as he heads toward the sound of his mother's voice, the clapping of her hands. He will need more time to get familiar with walking about while holding onto furniture, or holding someone's hands, and with standing by himself without holding on. He may also need more comforting and holding from his parents at this time, as if he were storing up an extra supply to take with him on his heroic journey through space.

The delay in creeping was more of a puzzle. Why does a healthy blind baby who can sit well, stand when his hands are held, and balance on hands and knees, take so long to move forward on all fours? There is no single answer to the question.

Part of the problem is that he has never seen other people moving from one place to another. Another factor is that he is moving into a total unknown, since he can't tell what lies ahead until he gets there. Creeping also demands a rather tricky coordination of arms and legs. It seemed to us, however, that an important part of the answer lay in another delay we have already mentioned — the fact that the blind baby does not begin reaching for what he hears until four or five months after the sighted baby has been reaching for what he sees.

For months the sighted baby has been stretching his arms toward what is out there ahead of him. On hands and knees at last, he reaches out again and finds himself suddenly on his stomach, but he can see that he is closer to his goal. Gradually his technique improves and he creeps expertly, learns not to reach for something too far away until he has moved within range. For the blind baby things are more complicated. Working with fewer and less reliable clues, he has to connect the sound of a toy heard in the distance with the sound and touch of the toy he once held in his hand and realize that he can touch it again, if only he can figure out how to get it. When he is on hands and knees and reaches out and lands on his stomach he has no way of telling that he has made progress. The sound is still "out there," and he is still "here." It takes the energy and eternal hopefulness of a growing child to persevere in such discouraging circumstances. And it takes time.

This period is a difficult one for the parents of a blind baby. It is hard not to worry about his slowness which comes at an age when sighted babies are moving ahead so rapidly. It is natural to wonder whether he will be slow in other ways too.

We try from the beginning to help parents anticipate and understand the possibility of these delays which are a normal stage for most blind children. We assure them that it has nothing to do with intelligence. We counsel patience and hope that parents will not try more than once or twice to move the baby's arms and legs to "make him creep," or to stand too far away to see if he will walk further faster. If the baby is made anxious he may stop trying completely, creating the very situation his parents fear.

It can be reassuring to review the good progress the baby has already made, the many signs of his love for his parents, confidence in himself, and active interest in the world around him. These are major accomplishments, based on months of effort by his parents to provide him with stimulation and activity.

The sighted baby is amazingly active in response to what he sees. His mother's smiling face, his own hands waving about, a moving shadow on the wall can start his arms and legs churning. Placed on his stomach he instantly raises his head in order to see better. He soon prefers sitting up to lying on his back, again getting a better view of the world. When he stands there are still more interesting sights. His interest in what he sees leads him to move from one position into another.

It is different for the blind baby. He does not have an infinite supply of enticing visual stimulation. He will be content to lie quietly on his back unless his parents help him find pleasure in activity, first with them, then by himself. The more often he experiences different positions through the day, the more used to them he will become. The more fun he has sitting for a pony ride, standing to pull his father's mustache, lying on his stomach across mommy's lap, the sooner he will hold himself well sitting, standing, and on his stomach. If he finds interesting things to play with while sitting, standing, and on his stomach, he will expect the world around him to be full of more interesting things, and, in time, will move ahead to find them. If he is accustomed to a variety of activities he will seek more.

It took what seemed like endless time for the babies to become mobile. But they did. And with mobility came greater independence and new discoveries. When Becky's mother went to the bedroom to diaper her baby sister, Becky crept after her, no longer left behind by herself. When Robbie did not want to stop playing outdoors at lunchtime he could run from his mother. One by one the children found the stack of magazines in the living room, the drawer with mother's curlers in the bedroom, the pots and pans in the kitchen cupboards.

Parents worry about the warning that their blind baby will rock all the time when he is older. People overlook the fact that there are many sighted children who enjoy rhythmic activity at some time in infancy. It can be a soothing activity, or a way to use up energy, or an experiment with the possibilities of balance and motion that gives the child interesting body sensations and information about himself. In the group of blind infants we followed some did not rock and some did for a while as a part of their normal development. It was most likely to occur after the baby was old enough to sit up, was used most frequently until the first birthday and decreased during the next year. We did not feel it was a cause for concern as long as the baby was making progress in other areas, was in touch with his mother and father and interested in the world outside himself. Bouncing seats, swings or rocking horses can be just as much fun for a blind child as for a sighted child when used to add variety to his activities during the day.

One other parental concern is that the blind baby will hurt himself when he starts to creep and then to walk. The children we knew collected the usual falls and bumps as they learned their way around the house. They needed the usual protection from stairways and sharp corners. But it was not necessary to rearrange the house nor to be right beside the adventurous blind baby all the time. A mother could keep an eye on things from a distance. She could protect the baby with her voice, warning him to "Slow down, the table is right in front of you." She could also, by voice, set some limits to his explorations, "I told you not to play with the new drapes." Of course, like any one or two year old, the blind baby would listen and obey, sometimes. At three and four he would be more responsive to prohibitions and more responsible.

Hands

A sighted baby's hands seem to be involved in almost everything he does. At first he can only hold tightly to one thing at a time, then two. When his grasp relaxes he can manage the double maneuver of holding and letting go, transferring a toy from one hand to the other. When there is nothing to play with he finds himself; his fingers explore the inside of his mouth, try to keep hold of his wriggly toes, or one hand discovers the other. He uses his hands to bring toys to his mouth to suck or to feel; later he brings food to his mouth, first to investigate, then to feed himself. His hands help him to creep, to pull up, to walk. As he picks up, pokes, bangs, and throws whatever comes within reach he is learning about texture and shape, weight, motion, and sound.

It is not only possible for the blind child to do all these things at nearly the same ages as sighted children, it is essential. To make up for what he has lost by not being able to see, his hands (as well as his ears) must begin to bring him information as soon as possible, must unite sensory experiences, must let him be effective in initiating events for himself. He should have all kinds of knowledge "at his fingertips" when he enters school, and he will be an apt pupil if he has spent the preschool years learning through touch about the things that make a child's world interesting, and that make him interesting to others.

We know from our studies that this does not happen automatically. Touch and hearing do not instantly substitute when sight is lost. Once again the blind baby is dependent upon his mother and father. Without their understanding of the problem, without their help, his hands may remain separate and solitary, closed to the experience he so badly needs and cannot seek by himself. A crucial path to discovery of the rich variety in the external world around him will be shut off.

New babies usually hold their hands fisted and up at the shoulder. The blind baby may continue to keep his hands at his shoulders for many months if he is not encouraged to lower his arms, to bring his hands to the center of his body, to the midline in front of his chest. With this in mind we make several suggestions to parents and call their attention to the importance of good hand development from the very start. Some have been described in the sections on toys and on self-feeding.

One of the simplest ways to bring the baby's hands to the midline and to offer them gentle stimulation is during a feeding in his mother's arms. After the first intense hunger subsides, the baby relaxes to finish his milk. Then his hands can be placed on the bottle and he can "look around" with his fingers. Soon he will recognize that the bottle he feels in his mouth and the bottle he feels with his hand are one and the same. He will notice that there are different sensations when he touches his own hand and when he touches his mother's. He will find the different textures of skin and clothing and bottle. All this while he is comfortably close to his mother, guided by her way of holding him, soothed by her voice. If he were alone with a propped bottle he would have to lie very still in order not to lose the nipple, his hands could not be active, there would be nothing to interest him. He would be deprived of necessary contact with his mother and of sensory stimulation as well.

There are other times when a baby's hands can be brought together in play, so that the movement of his arms toward the midline, and the feeling of one hand against the other become frequent and familiar occurrences. When he is being handled for bathing or dressing it is easy to "clap hands" with him. Most babies also enjoy lap games like "patty-cake," games that have an accompanying rhyme and that can be played with an adult who leads the way into a repeated pattern of voice and hand motions.

Variety of experience is another consideration. Rattles and bells to shake are all right for a while but we want to introduce the baby to new possibilities. We searched the stores for toys that would require different kinds of hand actions to produce a sound. With the baby's hand resting on ours we showed him how they worked. Now he had to pay close attention to the new toy in his hand. This one would not jingle just because he wanted it to, or because he waved his arm. He had to remember, or experiment and find out again how to squeeze or punch or wind it. He had to treat each toy differently. He could not expect them all to be the same. He was learning to find his way in unfamiliar situations.

Hand coordination and tactile discrimination are skills that are most easily established in the first eighteen months in harmony with the maturation and learning of the sensorimotor period. Watching the children in our research group grow up we became ever more aware of how much and in how many ways they were "seeing" with their hands.

Paul, at one year, had invented a trick: using his battered old cradle gym that still hung across the playpen, he pulled himself to a firm stand in the middle of nowhere, then swayed to and fro in a precarious balance, quite pleased with himself. When we looked at the film of Paul's trapeze act someone said, "Look at his fingers." At the same time that he was balancing and listening to his mother's delighted praise his index fingers were poking inquisitively into the holes on top of the cradle gym bar, noticing new details.

Karen, at eighteen months, was a picture of absorbed attention when we gave her a pastry brush to examine by herself. With a delicate touch Karen found all there was to know about the new object. She felt the hole in the smooth plastic handle, the twisted wire stem, the prickly bristles and the hollow metal cap that kept them in place. She shook the brush and the loosened cap clattered. Her face lit up with a smile. This was a fascinating treasure.

The inquiring fingers of Karen, Paul, and the others lead them to many discoveries. This early development of fine motor skills would become even more important for learning in school. Teachers of the blind, seeing films of these children, commented on their apparent reading readiness at ages three and four. Elizabeth can recognize her own long name in Braille as she comes to the end of her kindergarten year.

Language

"Will he learn to talk?"

"Yes."

The blind children in the group we studied were able to say their first words, recognize their names and understand no-no at the same age as sighted children; at two and three years they were able to speak just as clearly as sighted children of the same age. By four and five years the children in our group were generally as articulate and outspoken as other children their age. Elizabeth and Karen and Paul and most of the others spoke their minds. They were humorous or angry, questioning or understanding, stubborn or delightfully charming.

Since we know that the use of language is a tremendously complicated process influenced and aided in many ways by vision, the good achievements of these blind children are truly remarkable. Still we are not surprised to find some differences and delays. Sighted babies want and reach for what they see on sight by four to six months. Not until several months later does a blind baby show us he knows of and wants things that are not at his fingertips. The blind child can sit and stand when the sighted child can — but is delayed by as much as five to seven months in creeping and walking, needing that time to practice and prepare, and to learn that space is not empty, but is furnished with interesting objects that make the effort of the journey worthwhile. Now we also find that the blind child is ready to speak at approximately the same time as the sighted child, but takes longer to expand his vocabulary, to construct more complex sentences, to untangle the pronouns, to use past and future tenses. It seems to us to be further confirmation that vision makes it relatively easy for the sighted child at every step of the way.

The blind child cannot read the gestures and facial expressions that give added meaning to what we say. He cannot summon up a visual image of what he is trying to recall and name. He cannot easily size up a situation at a glance, or see and understand instantly the relationship between people and himself, the distances between things. In use of language the blind child does catch up with the sighted child by four or five years, but for him the task is more difficult, his success that much greater.

What can a mother and father do to help their blind baby learn to speak? If they have been holding and talking to their baby, letting him know their voices, his learning has already begun. Speaking to him before he is picked up lets him anticipate what is coming. Talking to him about what is happening, what is going to happen, accompanying actions with words, naming the toy or bottle or whatever he is feeling will build voices and words into the total experience of being cared for. At first the sound of pleasant voices arouses his interest. Soon he will begin recognizing patterns in the sounds and eventually understand the meanings of the words themselves: "Here is your bottle." "Hold still while I wipe your face." "Let's play patty-cake." Words will begin to bring him information about objects, himself, and others. A baby makes his own sounds, cooings and babblings and cries. If parents respond to his first vocalizations then his own sound production enters into the "conversation." This may not yet be what we mean by language, but it represents a start.

Children usually understand more than we give them credit for. The alert blind child has reason to listen carefully to what is said around him since he gets so many of his cues from the words of others. We can never measure all of his understanding, but we can see in his response to requests or commands that he comprehends the meaning of what is said, that he appreciates the power of the spoken word. Becky reluctantly gives up a forbidden plaything when her mother calls out, "Put the lighter back on the table. You know that's not something to play with." When Paul can't make his musical toy start, he encourages himself by saying, "Pull it! Pull it!" and when his small fingers do manage the complicated mechanism at last, he pats himself on the back by telling himself, "Good boy."

Blind children may need to use repetition as a memory aid more than sighted children do. It will drop out as spontaneous speech takes over. Another difference we have found is that blind children at three and four years of age are less interested in listening to stories than sighted children of the same age. It takes longer for blind children to build up their own store of firsthand adventures; more time before they will be ready to tell about themselves, more time before they will like tales of other children or animals or giants and goblins.

In the interim the blind child can get great pleasure from songs and rhymes and ABC and number chants, especially when they are sung or recited as part of an activity with a favorite person. Bath songs and bed songs and "1-2-3 jump!" and silly nonsense songs all encourage him to join in. Elizabeth had a wealth of songs to choose from. She could be heard singing and talking to herself before she fell asleep, using words to hold on to the day a little longer.

Eventually, experience and ideas and the overall balance of development fitted together and the children moved ahead more rapidly in their use of language. Parents announced, "It's wonderful. Now we can have real conversations with Richie." Our own notes would read, "Almost impossible to record everything. Becky was talking all the time." The last signs of infancy were left behind. The babies had become assertive and confident little boys and girls. They had questions and answers and funny things to say. They had opinions to express and imaginative ideas too. Listening to what the children said we could get glimpses of the ways in which they were making sense of the world. "A nut is something like an egg," says Elizabeth. "Why?" we ask. "You crack it," is her prompt reply. There are egg shells and sea shells; they are the same and different. Elizabeth plays around with that intriguing thought. She is looking for relationships, similarities and differences. She is generalizing and classifying, creating order from her experience.

School

"Hey Mom! Let's go. This is a school day."

In jeans or jumpers, in snowsuits or light jackets the children are out the door with mother close behind. It *is* time to go to school. The blind babies have grown up and they are ready to spend part of the day away from home. The decision about when to start nursery school or kindergarten is an individual one for each child. Some sighted children are ready before the usual age, some after. The same is true for the blind child. He will be ready for school when he is able to tolerate separation from home and mother for short periods; when he has shown that he can share an adult's attention with other children; when he has a good command of language both for understanding others and for making himself understood. By four and five years the blind children we followed were mature enough to manage well in a group of other four and five year olds.

Like the sighted child, the well-stimulated blind child has been learning since infancy. He has a wealth of information and understanding about his small part of the world. He knows about indoors and outdoors, upstairs and down, "right away" and "in a little while." Faucets and radios turn on and off. Refrigerators open and close and are cold inside and that is where to find the chocolate syrup. Toasters get hot and go pop and the bread feels different before and after you put it in. It is all right to bounce on the old armchair in the hall, but not on the living room davenport. He is beginning to have his own interests and ideas and sometimes wants to be by himself to concentrate on a tinker toy construction, or just to fool around in the basement. He can hold his own in the give-and-take of play with other children. He no longer needs constant and undivided attention from his parents.

The larger world of school lies ahead. There the teacher will become his guide and support. Her role in the classroom will be as central to the blind child as his parents' role will continue to be at home. Confident, alert, and active, the blind boy or girl has been well prepared for the new learning and new friendships to be found at school.

Different educational resources were available in the communities where the children that we knew lived. Elizabeth was welcomed by the teacher of a regular nursery school. Other children entered a Headstart program, nursery school classes for the handicapped, nursery schools for the blind. We continued to make home visits and occasionally were able to go to the schools to observe, take films, and speak to the teachers.

Most teachers of small children have special gifts of warmth, patience, and ingenuity. But several of the men and women we spoke with were unfamiliar with very young blind children. They drew upon their past teaching experience, their understanding of child development and of the learning process to meet the unique needs of the blind child in their classes. It was important for them to know in what ways normal development for the blind child was similar to and different from that of the sighted child in order to plan realistically. If the blind child were "treated just like any child," the teacher's inevitable doubt about her own effectiveness would be felt by the child as disappointment in him. Questions arose for the teachers, just as they had earlier for the parents. Over a period of time, as we combined our own observations of the children with those of the families and the teachers, we found the answers.

The blind child who can find his way around his house and yard, who has been walking in the neighborhood, to the park or downtown, knows how to get around, but he still needs time to learn a new place. If he is to be independent in school the simplest way is to let him map the room for himself ahead of time. He will have trouble finding his bearings when the room is full of children if he doesn't already have some sense of where things are. Many teachers invite mother and child to come to school for a short visit by themselves before the term begins. This is an ideal arrangement for the blind child. His mother can introduce him to the teacher. His teacher can introduce him to the room, showing him the major landmarks, the doorway, the toy shelves, the play table, the piano. When he returns as a member of the group he will be better oriented. The blind child can make his way in the classroom if the other children are not too helpful, if he is not hurried along, if he is permitted to find his own route with just enough unambiguous direction from the teacher. "Let's all sit on the rug near the piano," is clearer than "Come over here now."

Children transfer to their teachers the trust and some of the affection they bear for their parents. In the stimulating and sometimes confusing classroom scene the teacher is a reliable source of protection and information. The sighted child can keep track of her whenever he wants to, by looking up from his play to see where she is or what she is doing. She glances at him too and he knows that she is aware of him. The presence of teacher and child and their relationship to each other has been reaffirmed with no break in the flow of activity. The blind child also needs to know that his teacher is there and that she cares about him. Since he cannot see her he interrupts his play to call her name. She can offer reassuring recognition to the blind child by saying his name, telling him where she is, by finding many small ways to let him know by her voice and touch that she is there and that she is aware of him. Without this he will feel lost. He needs her very much, more than the sighted child does. This places extra demands on the teacher's sensitivity and inventiveness and is difficult to manage without an assistant or with too large a group. It will take the blind child longer to size things up, to become familiar with the room, the children, each new object and activity. And for that longer period the teacher will have to help him verbally and physically. She will have to provide ways to combine concrete experience with words, to offer reliable cues and comprehensible directions to supply in other means what vision makes so effortlessly available to the rest of the class. Unlike Elizabeth, who was totally blind, some of the children were able to perceive light or color. Even this small amount of visual stimulation was an advantage that could be capitalized on by an aware teacher.

119

Given the right cues and enough time, with a minimum of interfering overprotection and just enough gentle assistance, the blind children we have worked with have done well in school. Their good language skills and good gross motor and fine motor coordination enabled them to take part in almost anything that did not rely completely on vision. They spoke well and used language for sophisticated social exchange sooner than many sighted children. They completed what they started more often than their sighted classmates, perhaps because they were less readily distracted. They held fast in squabbles over toys and taking turns.

We began to hear stories of spunk and determination. In the playroom Paul found the jungle gym and climbed to the top. With help he swooped down the attached slide, and immediately had to climb back up — but up the slide, not the ladder. It was carefully explained to him that the ladder was the only way to get to the top. Paul stubbornly tried, as children always have, to get some kind of purchase on the slippery smoothness, while the adults patiently repeated, as they always have, that it couldn't be done. And then Paul did it. He placed his rubber-soled shoes on the slide and up he went.

Each child needs to try some things on his own. He also wants to do what the other boys and girls are doing, to sing the same songs, to make a paper fan, to bring something to Show and Tell. Following the example set by the teacher the children in the class accept the blind child as one of themselves and come to join him, hitching a ride on the back of his trike, whispering secrets. They include him in their own play, but the teachers report that the blind child is less likely to seek the other children. It is not only that he can't always tell whether they are doing something that would interest him. The blind child will frequently separate from the group, as if he needs time to be by himself.

The wise teacher respects this need, understanding that children can learn when they are being quiet as well as when they are active. The teacher who has been devoting so much care to helping the blind child advance into new experience also has to let him step back from it. It must never be forgotten that although the blind child is older now and doing so well, learning without vision is harder. It is an effort for a small boy or girl to have to give careful and selective attention to an unforeseeable whirl of stimulation and information. What he must do is much more difficult than what the sighted child is doing, especially since the world is set up for the sighted. The blind child needs time out to relax from constant alertness. He also needs time to think about what has just happened in order to strengthen a memory, since he does not have a visual image to help him recall the scene.

Children use imaginative play to help themselves remember, to reenact and to anticipate events. Pretending with dolls, with miniature tea sets, or small cars and trucks occurs later for the blind child than it does for the sighted. Once again we must understand, and provide him with opportunities to become thoroughly familiar with the actual qualities and functions of things and let him take time to observe himself in relation to them. Only then can he enjoy the freedom from absolute fact, and the control over what was and what might be that comes with imagination. The fact that the delightful inventive play that occupies the sighted child from two years on may not occur for the blind child until he is three or four tells us how fundamental the role of vision can be in this area of development.

The last time I visited Elizabeth, she took me outdoors to look for the house of her imaginary friend, Zeen. I was in the dark as to where we might be going, but Elizabeth seemed confident. She led me through dense brush, down a slope and over the broad lawn. Although it was a damp, windy day Elizabeth was in no hurry to shorten the adventure. When I developed the sniffles she thoughtfully produced a make-believe tissue and wiped my nose, encouraging me to go a little further to see what we could find. Zeen never turned up. He had just been a good excuse for us to go exploring together. We investigated the ice on a puddle, the logs in the woodpile, and the sandbox, while Elizabeth chatted about old friends she remembered at The Project. Then we returned to the warm house where Elizabeth exchanged a hug and a kiss with her mother and I bid them good-bye.

Edna Adelson
Research Psychologist with
the Child Development Project
at The University of Michigan